Evil and Greed

Leon Reed Adams, Ph.D.

Cover Illustrator:
Sgt. William C. Hoffman

To order additional copies of this book, contact:
Xlibris
844-714-8691
www.Xlibris.com
Orders@Xlibris.com
823632

CONTENTS

Acknowledgements and Dedication

"Radix malorum est cupiditas" is Latin for "the root of evil is greed", and we agree. This book is dedicated to all those throughout history who have labored to understand evil and greed in all its forms, and to those who have battled evil and greed. Particular recognition is devoted to Ms. Judith Helms and Ms. Nell Adams who have demonstrated a lifetime of virtuous and altruistic behaviors, illustrating a vital theoretical component of the study of behavior. Special appreciation is acknowledged for the support and encouragement provided by the following exceptionally helpful readers: Ms. Adelaida de Guzman, Mrs. Judy Renshaw, Mr. Tyler Helms, Ms. Emily Kukackaemily, Mrs. Patricia Boelte, Mr. Ed Boelte, and Mrs. Judith Adams Helms. Mrs. Christine Wilson served an exceptional role as a reader and as a librarian providing highly competent academic skills and encouragement. Mrs. Risa Hall served as our excellent typist. Mr. William Hoffman served as our exceptionally talented illustrator and much more. He was an advisor, consultant, and source of encouragement without equal. This project would not have been completed without the individuals noted above. God bless all of you.

PART ONE

DESCRIPTIONS, DEFINITIONS AND PATTERNS.

Chapter One

GREED AND EVIL DEFINED AND OPERATIONALIZE

Chapter One

Greed and Evil Defined and Operationalized

The King James Version of the Bible states that "the love of money is the root of all evil" (or all kinds of evil). Clearly, money is linked intimately with greed and evil, although it is not linked in every case of evil. This book is devoted to an exploration of all types of evil and their causes. The primary causes of greatest concern herein are greed and hate of others unlike us. Obviously, other causes, such as psychopathy or mental illness, can create evil. Here we take the position that those intentional and purposeful human actions causing pain and suffering of any type, be it physical, mental, emotional, fiscal, political, or whatever, are evil actions. We also address the obverse of evil as one method of comprehensively analyzing evil. In the process of the consideration of good and evil we highlight a contemporary, rare, perhaps unique, development linking of God and science. That is discussed after our full treatment of the variables involved.

We identify this work as interdisciplinary owing its formation from the ideas of many scientists across many academic disciplines. Our ideas are old, and our contribution is to the emphases we place. Much is to be gained from the continuing study of belonging to groups and the not yet fully developed dynamic of group involvement. The idea of belonging, of community, of the we-feeling, of gemeinschaft is based in sociology and social psychology. Critical to such analysis are such variables as "power", "rank", "status", "social ties", "social structure", "in-group", and "out-group". The allocation of rewards and punishments is typically a dynamic aspect of "Evil". The dynamics of In-Group interactions with Out-Groups are the fundamental theoretical variables we argue are typically critical for the causation of evil. The model we suggest is that presented by Masey discussed below. A dynamic often involved in evil acts includes the positive and rewarding values, norms and actions within one's In-Group and the opposite with one's Out-Group. Keep in mind much variation of all variables may be expected.

Figure One: In-Group/Out-Group Interactions

Table One: Validity or Invalidity of the Prevailing Scientific Model related to research cited		
	Scientific evidence shows new model of consciousness	**Scientific evidence shows only measurable human conditions**
TRUE	**New scientific philosophy and paradigm**	**Existing scientific model unchanged**
FALSE	**Prevailing scientific model prevails and remains**	**New scientific philosophy and paradigm**

See below for the discussion of Robert K. Merton's theory, as an especially relevant discussion for our theoretical focus.

Our review of research and theory has left us with the awareness that the effects of our social definitions and identifications ("others") as members of specific groups plays a more profound role than is generally recognized. We may be oblivious to our own In/Group | Out/Group values and norms, allowing actions based on our social assumptions to be evil in their impact. That was the surprising finding of research at the University of Washington[1]. Those researchers studied fifty **(50!)** years of scientific studies and found that favoritism towards friends based on traits such as race, age, gender, and religion was a common event. Their recognized exclusions were based on the others being "unlike us", as we argue herein. Bernstein defines in/groups - out/groups as "Humans benefit from living in groups, and this results in social organization consisting of in/groups and out/groups. In/groups are the groups to which individuals both belong and psychologically identify, while out-groups are those to which individuals do not belong or identify. Categorizations based on In/Group–Out/Group distinctions have a profound impact on social interactions, including aspects of prejudice, reward allocation, stereotyping, and group conflict."[2]

A critical element of evil is "purpose". Evil can be created by a sociopath without regard to the effects or consideration other than desire and self-interest, or it simply occurs to him/her to do it. Evil though that action may be, particularly with reference to repercussions beyond the victim, we do not define it as the level of evil perpetuated by someone intending to bring about identical affects and outcomes. Thus, the same outcomes may vary by intent and purpose, so that a hierarchy of evil may be seen.

It is critical for the reader to recognize this monograph as a multipurpose essay. Hopefully, this work will generate functional links between science and social policy. Also we intend for this to serve as a textbook in criminology and other social science classes as well as a more general review of research and theory. Moreover, we wish for this to serve as an avenue to creative conceptualization of abstract ideas and religious / philosophical considerations. Thus, this work is an interdisciplinary social and behavioral science monograph. Some topics are of such theoretical formulation we deal with them in a second volume. Our present authors represent several academic disciplines and scientific perspectives. We feel this is required by the wide-ranging manner humanity has handled the subject of "evil" throughout history.

While "evil" is clearly one of the most important topics of human existence, it has not been an adequately researched scientific subject. This is true even in our field of Criminology and Criminal Justice. The reluctance of scientists and philosophers to address "evil" as a variable and as a subject for scientific study is apparent from a simple review of the social and behavioral science literature. This academic and scientific condition was profoundly recognized as noted herein by a brilliant scientific paper from the University of York in the UK. The perception of that scholar, Aliraza Javaid[3], and the far-reaching / empirical radical implications of his work for science and for humanity by his broaching of "evil" as a scientific subject cannot be overemphasized[4]. His is a scientific perception of the highest order. Javaid placed "evil" as a social science concept in perspective, acknowledging that humanity (including scientists and philosophers) have ignored "evil". He acknowledged the dearth of scientific studies relevant to our present concerns, arguing that sociologists have "abandoned" the topic. Properly claiming that his interdisciplinary effort linking multiple perspectives in the conceptualization of the scientific concept "evil" is "original", he leads the way to the innovative study such as herein discussed. Recognizing the scientific inadequacy of our disciplines to operationalized "evil" in all its forms, he focused on pedophilia as an example. That seminal paper addressed the operationalization of evil as more than simply acts that are wrong or bad. Going beyond "bad" he sees "evil" as a condition that cannot coexist with a good God, and takes the reader into a discussion of religion and sociology. Arguing that "evil" is socially and culturally constructed, he theorizes that such acts must be seen from the perspective of the offender's values and norms.

1. Social science and religion need not conflict conceptually, but may complement one another. An important point is the recognition that evil acts and evil people may work in a larger perspective to the greater good for all. Thus, God is not logically dismissed by the argument that evil cannot coexist with God.

2. Critical variables can be identified. Javaid discusses the primary theoretical models used to quantify reality and "evil". The forces used by theorists have been (a) cultural, (b) social (that is, institutional / situational), (c) individual qualities (both learned and inherited), and (d) supernatural (God and the devil). A and B argue that acts are evil, not individuals. Thus "good people" can commit "evil" acts. Javaid also identifies In-Group / Out-Group values, consistent with the theme of this essay. He argues "evil" is socially and culturally created, so that "evil" people are unique to their culture.

Building upon such as the Javaid work, we attempt an operationalization of "evil" that social scientists might use in research and conceptualization. Javaid made the following points, relevant to our interdisciplinary model. Directly in line with this text, Rosenbaum[5] sees "evil" as defined by the degree of harm and the intent of the actor. Thus, a person may be seen as creating great harm but if the motive was not evil, it is lower on the hierarchy of "evil".

"Greed" is commonly known to everyone, but not typically as a scientific concept. Yet, it is certainly subject to scientific scrutiny[6]. One model describes greed as having two primary elements: the rewarding experience of gaining something, and the guilt from having acted in a selfish fashion, with "desirability, guilt, and empathetic perspective taking" being the most powerful components[7]. Those scientists point out that greed has appeared throughout human history, and is a common element of human character, even being a critical issue with Plato and Socrates[8]. Yet their review of the scientific literature on greed found that surprisingly little empirical research has been done. Humanity does not see greed in all its forms as evil, for greed is simply a form of self-interest typically acknowledged as acceptable. By self-interest, we mean the need to achieve, to maximize material gains and to minimize losses. Indeed this concept is central to most economic models. Moreover, it is widely acknowledged that greed can produce positive, good and desirable outcomes. It has been argued that greed can and often does produce more social good than benevolence[9] or selfishness for the social virtues, that is, the common good. Karl Marx[10], as one would expect, saw greed as an evil part of capitalism, and as such should be rejected. A review of greed in the literature (Balot, ibid) concluded that greed contains vice and excess as essential qualities, and as such is evil. Such also overlaps with *schadenfreude*, a German concept for taking joy at the suffering of others[11]. A very important point has been made by a witness to the trial of Nazi leader Adolph Eichmann. That scholarly observer, Hannah Arendt[12] argued that evil is common, found throughout humankind, and occurs when social circumstances cause or allow otherwise normal humans to re-defined social conditions and even redefine other humans. Certainly this is consistent with our review of the prison experiment of Zimbardo (see below, section on Social Structure and recent critical reviews of that experiment and our focus on In/Group and Out/Group).

As will be seen in our description of the Church of Satan, some persons act on the assumption and firm belief that the supernatural, including evil spirits, are as real as other aspects of our physical world. Readers wishing to review vivid descriptions of such activities should see the work of Gerald Brittle. That frightening work reviews by interview the activities and function of Demonologists and others dealing with the supernatural. They offer services as investigators, counselors and lecturers. At Southern Connecticut State College, they offer a course in "Demonology and Paranormal Phenomena". The academic work cited below is a review of psychic activity of primarily evil spirits, including photographs of their activity as the spirits destroy the physical world of humanity. They deal in detail with the theological relationship of our God with Lucifer. The evidence they present is substantial if their assumptions are taken as true. The function of this monograph is to describe and assess the evil than humans do, yet there is overlap as the devils described by Brittle and many others links to evil human behavior, though not the primary function of devils. As (devils) are not at this time receptive to empirical test and empirical measurement, it is difficult to address beyond our acknowledgement of the existence of such. For a discussion of the logic underlying non-physical variables, see our section on theology and evil.

It is our purpose to stimulate academic / intellectual considerations of evil, involved both with theory and research, with an emphasis on the role of "group" variables. Any such effort must encourage readers to see the work of Michael Stone. His <u>Anatomy of Evil</u>, (see footnote 13), is a "must read" for those attempting an understanding of evil. His elaboration of a definition of evil identifies the multiple abstractions involved. He argues the best definition of evil is what the people identify as such. We agree and have included in this manuscript an appendix of such data. It is unusual, perhaps unique, in the data collection strategies and research design. That data has not been analyzed, and the reader may use it as they wish, hopefully, to draw attention to our focused theory of In/Groups/Out-Groups.

Stone[13] (see above) offers a working definition of evil as situations or humans acts involving significant injury. Such must involve four elements:

1. Breathtakingly horrible
2. Malice aforethought
3. Excessive suffering
4. Incomprehensible

Stone's work addresses empirical scales of evil and a comprehensive analysis/description of the various categories of evil. Readers are emphatically encouraged to read his seminal work. Fascinating in the extreme, his work provides detailed case histories categorized by type. His analysis covers the entire range of analytic exploration, including psychiatric, psychological, physiological, genetic, and medical.

Chapter Two
Others Unlike Us: Distrust and Hate

CHAPTER TWO

Others Unlike Us: Distrust and Hate

Below we review, in a limited fashion, some characterizations of the "Outsider" variable. It appears it existed from very early human times and continues to flourish today. Indeed there may even be a genetic predisposition to have friends like ourselves, as reported by the National Academy of Sciences.[14] Noting that the tendency of humans to have friends similar in looks dates from the time of Plato, the report indicated our friends are as close genetically as fourth cousins. That the aggressive propensity towards those in other groups is ancient is shown by research on a prehistoric massacre reported in the journal "Nature". It reports that the discovery of 12 apparently bound human skeletons over 10,000 years old indicates "…intergroup conflict may extend much deeper into our evolutionary past".

A theoretically wide-ranging and intellectually expansive analysis of how evil and good developed can be found in the works of Bloom.[15] Basing his theoretical concepts in reason, research, theology and philosophy, he argues we come into the word as babies with a sense of morality yet it evolves as we age so that ultimately we are a moral animal formed from several sources. Readers please note the primary theoretical focus of our work involves the contribution that normal, "everyday" type people make to evil events. Indeed, the apparent normality of many evil people is a critical basis of our argument for the impact of group identity. The death and suffering of World War II was carried out by people whose lives were often primarily normal. An unusual treatment of the backgrounds of those playing important roles in WWII has been produced as an almanac of the Holocaust[16]. That work outlines the lives as well as the evil and other actions of the primary actors of WWII, politicians and beyond.

ELABORATION OF EVIL

The dearth of academic research around the theory of evil, its operationalization, and empirical studies is reversed in the theological considerations of evil. Yet, while there are considerable treatments of religion and evil, there can yet be more. Some works have been profound and insightful, but the theology of evil is beyond the primary focus of this book. A section of our effort has been to attempt a description of theology and evil. We may also provide identification of some works we believe are poignant, highly relevant and critical in their identification of religion / evil as a topic. Interested readers should see our citations and the second volume of our work yet to be released. Of course, serious students of theology and evil should begin with a focused study of the Bible. Attention must be called to the 7 deadly sins, anger, envy, covetousness, gluttony, lust, pride, and sloth.

Greed appears in human affairs so often it is taken for granted. Moreover, as greed (self-interest) is a ubiquitous human trait, we tend to be more accepting of it than other evils. Yet, our argument here is to look beyond and below the obvious human behaviors and question the development and maintenance of greed and other forms of evil.

Sometimes greed can be harmful to others beyond the perpetrator, yet not be illegal or be questionable. We note that actions by some our leaders, both political and business leaders, have repeatedly caused harmful outcomes that meet the definition of "evil". Many scholars consider the book *Pigs at the Trough*[17] (a New York Times bestseller) to be one of the best descriptions of the deplorable and extensively harmful financial debacle that hit America in the early 2000s. The financial crisis of 2007–09 is considered by many economists to be the worst financial crisis since the *Great Depression*[18]. Arianna Huffington describes it as "...the lunatic excesses and the frenzy of fraud perpetrated by our high flying corporate chieftains have left America's 401(k)s and pension plans in ruins and more than 8 million people out of work."[19] She noted that in a one year period of that evil time 1 ½ million people filed for bankruptcy, investors lost $9 trillion, and retirement assets lost 11% of their value, or $630 billion. She also points out this happened because of the collaboration of our politicians with the corporation leaders. Moreover, she directly names the lobbyists, politicians and business leaders, with the companies involved. To emphasize the evil involved in many ways she notes "Billion dollar corporations continue to ride first class on the government gravy train while, even in the middle of a recession, desperate measures like temporary welfare assistance for needy families have been given the boot"[20]

Morgenson and Rosner, of the ***New York Times***, reported on the interaction of political positions with financial establishment positions so as to allow greed and evil to cause "economic Armageddon"[21]. They discuss how those in positions of trust so as to protect the public were involved and contributed to the mortgage crisis that harmed so many people. Not only do they identify the structural elements, but also name people and positions preventing the public protection assumed to be in place by so many. They even provide pictures of the individuals at the heart of the debacle.

An excellent review of patterns of greed may be found in Balleisen's work "Fraud: An American History from Barnum to Madoff"[22]. Delving into the history of dishonest business dealings, he illustrates how "fraud" has evolved and our changing response to it. Discussing the millions of instances of identity theft and internet based scams, he demonstrates the relevance of the study of fraud and greed in today's world. The argument is presented that fraud in America has gone through four policy phases, with the current phase marking continued evidence of greed and dishonesty. This continues despite the apparent efforts of some legislators to regulate business through honorable and honest policy.

We argue herein that the ancient phenomena of disliking and distrusting those outside our own "group" and trusting those within our group may be argued to be the most important causal factor in evil, greed and hate. It is not, we maintain, that scientists have failed to recognize the existence and potential of this force, but that it has not been given adequate scientific attention or acknowledged as the power it represents. This failing to address other groups' hate may be because it hits home, we all do it. We argue that the operation of this variable is ignored by most people, including many scientists, theorists, theologians, and philosophers. Moreover, the interaction of this force with other forces demands study in order that we may approach a comprehensive understanding of evil. Also, we must address our social policies/laws. Entire academic disciplines are devoted to the study of groups, but less so to the study of In/Group-Out/Group invisibility. Those finding it difficult to accept pervasive mistreatment based on this variable should start by a consideration of gender, and see that women age 51-64 are paid 38% less than men[23]. Also, consider the "#metoo

Movement." Then, look within yourself and ask if your own reactions have ever been anger.

A profoundly insightful description and analysis of America today has been provided by U.S. senator, Dr. Ben Sasse. His book documents in vivid fashion his assertion that "we are living through an economic and social revolution that is transforming the life we have known for a century and a half. We need to be able to name this moment, and we need to be clear-eyed enough to admit that the challenges this moment presents are not going to be solved by government: they can't be."[24] The "cries" he describes are consistent with the clash of In-Group/Out-Group we argue are fundamental to a theoretical evil group. Our social definitions of "THEM" as evil can be resolved by manipulation of our In-Group norms. He states, "… It's not legislation we are lacking; it is the tight bonds that give our lives meaning, happiness, and hope. It's the habits of heart and mind that make use of neighbors and friends. At the end of the day, it's love. When a bunch of 'them' are joined by love and by purpose, 'they' can become 'we'."[25]

A further interpretation of our review of research findings by other scientists regarding the early origins of war stated that "Lethal raids by competing groups were part of life for hunter-gatherer communities…" and that warfare between "bands of stone-age people" may go back as far as 60,000 years, and that "group identities" may have begun as long as 2 million years ago[26]. Thus, such evidence suggests the "In/Group | Out/Group" variable may be an "original" trait of humans. Morrow[27] references the anthropological study of the Gahuku-Gama people in New Guinea showing their concept of morality and norms was based on the notion of others. Those not part of their group were not considered human. Morrow's work well identifies the relativism of evil. Acts in one context may be evil but the same acts in other circumstances are not.

Consider also the community reaction causing the Salem Witch Trials[28]. As Marilynne Roach shows in detailed description of the events leading to the execution of "witches," it is clear the community redefined "witches" as a specific "Out-Group."

What is considered by some as the most profound theoretical formulation of In-Group/ Out-Group theory appeared in *American Psychologist*. In that paper Greenwald and Pettigrew identify the failure of scientists to adequately recognize the importance and role of an ignored element of group theory, "favoritism"[29] . Their seminal paper focuses on interpersonal discrimination, but their theory is sufficiently broad as to incorporate multiple aspects of human behavior. "In-Group Preferential Treatment", easily recognized in all human lives, is set forth as a more powerful cause of discrimination than Out-Group hostility. Indeed, they agree that discrimination does not require hostility. Such favoritism may even be unintentional and unrecognized by the decision maker. In-Group favoritism thus becomes the prime cause of discrimination. Their critical theoretical elements, (1) positive assessment of fellow In-Group members and (2) equal or greater social force of favoritism over hostility, are buttressed by cited research. Yet, despite the theoretical potency of favoritism, it has been largely ignored. A powerful aspect of their theoretical formulation involves the similarity and attraction component. They assert that even when these are at play, the most powerful determinant is not specific shared attributes, but rather the membership in the same In-Group. Their influential paper explored the theoretical issues from multiple perspectives, determining that "Our strong conclusion is that, in present-day America, discrimination results more from helping in-group members than from harming out-group members"[30]. Readers, especially those addressing issues of discrimination, are strongly encouraged to review their work.

Substantial value to the scientific formulation of greed, evil and the socially structured causes of it lies in the work of David Rothkopf[31]. He presents a valid analysis of the "Superclass," the "In/Group" controlling world economics and political power. His work is a clear demonstration of our focus on "In/Group", and the dynamics of the variables involved. Moreover, his analysis shows the vital importance of our focus.

Isenberg argued that "Rationalizing economic inequality has been an unconscious part of the national credo...poor whites had to be classified as a distinct breed..."[32] Her argument that the creation of distinct groups of "other" humans has been an unconscious and ignored component of the sociological scene is consistent with the fundamental premise and theoretical elements of this book. Her work is emphatically endorsed, as is the work of Sora[33] who writes on the "hidden" activities of the groups of elites who make money and power from the creation and manipulation of "Out-Groups", and have done so from the beginning of our republic.

Race

One of the most evident group of people "not like us" in our modern world is the "other-race" groups. The operation of this variable creates a more visible anger than many other variables, even though social class, economic groups, and gender groups often equal or exceed race in their impact, or overlap with race. Moreover, the *interaction* of variables is more often seen in the interplay of non-race-based variables than in the case of race, which is often seen as standing alone. For these reasons it is vital that social scientists and policy makers make every possible effort to conceptualize "race" beyond its present limited variables. Given the profound and massive reconceptualization made by many scientists and also by public citizens as they struggled only a few decades ago to shift race as a genetic physiological concept to a social classification, we know such change is possible. Yet, much needs to be done to advance this as a research and policy issue. Our recent improved understanding of the nature of this variable deserves applause. We now know, for example, that there is more genetic diversity *within* a racial group than *between* two different racial groups[34]. Illustrating our ideas is an articulate description of the perspective of one racial group considering "white privilege". Their argument is consistent with this essay that "other" groups involve assumptions so strong they are often not understood by those using them.[35]

As this monograph illustrates, there is much social benefit to be gained from understanding the conditions underlying and causing evil and very much to be lost from ignoring such considerations. This section discusses one fundamental aspect of evil, certain sociological conditions in which evil occurs. Indeed, the point is made that "race" has historically been the basis of very much evil and it continues to so operate. "Race" as it is deployed in the world today concerns not only physiological conditions such as skin color and facial qualities, but the condition of being "Other" than the observer. Indeed, this broad variable remains as a highly significant social force today.[36] Moreover, it is well established that "race", as a biological variable indicating substantial differences such as intelligence, is not now a viable scientific concept, although it was only in the very recent past so accepted[37]. Rather, it is clear that differential association with various groups is fundamentally a sociological phenomenon. Are there differences among groups of humans that reflect different crime rates? Yes of course. Is that difference in crime rates "caused" by genetically determined qualities? No. There is no evidence to suggest the operation of such a physiological variable in such a fashion, although it is obvious that groups have such differences, such as skin color. And it is clear groups differ in social norms and values, causing them to differ in behavior, broadly construed. It is the difference in social norms and values that "causes" evil, not physiological conditions.

One of the more disturbing reports of In/Group – Out/Group effects can be seen from the medical treatments afforded black people. It involves medical experimentation as well as levels of medical treatment. An extensive treatment of those effects is provided by Harriet Washington's report[38]. The perception of blacks as an Out/Group different in ways common to the Nazi view of non-Aryans is clear.

Race and Intelligence were presented in a possibly unique (scientifically) book, *The Bell Curve*[39]. It is described as unique for it presented a discussion of a social issue of massive significance for humanity, especially the United States. The reaction of the scientific / academic community was genuinely unsettling, and unusually broad. One reviewer[40] stated *The Bell Curve* "created a firestorm of debate on the contribution of inherited intelligence to the success or failure of individuals in society". That understatement was correct, as book reviews, articles and entire books served as a rejoinder to *The Bell Curve*. Using the National Longitudinal Study of Youth (NLSY), *The Bell Curve* argues, with quite substantial science behind it, that IQ is inherited and is the primary "cause" of success, measured in multiple and socially important ways. Much of the agitation generated by the book was related to the argument that races differ in intelligence, with Asian cultures being highest and African Blacks being low. They argue we are headed for trouble in our society if we do not acknowledge the role of IQ. They warn we should anticipate

- "An increasingly isolated cognitive elite.
- A merging of the cognitive elite with the affluent.

- A deteriorating quality of life for people at the bottom end of the cognitive ability and distribution."[41]

Our concern is primarily with their treatment of evil and crime. Highly respected criminologists have written "By reanalyzing the data used in *The Bell Curve* and by reviewing existing meta-analyses assessing the relative importance of criminogenic risk factors, the present authors show empirically that Herrnstein and Murray's claims regarding IQ and crime are misleading. The authors conclude that Herrnstein and Murray's crime control agenda is based on ideology, not on intelligent criminology."[42] Politely put, this rejection of *The Bell Curve* is representative of a wide reaction within the scientific community. Some, not quoted here, were less polite. A recent review shows the authors stating: "There is a mean difference in black and white scores on mental tests, historically about one standard deviation in magnitude on IQ tests (IQ tests are normed so that the mean is 100 points and the standard deviation is 15). This difference is not the result of test bias, but reflects differences in cognitive functioning. The predictive validity of IQ scores for educational and socioeconomic outcomes is about the same for blacks and whites. Those were our confidently stated conclusions about the black-white difference in IQ, and none of them was scientifically controversial".[43] See the report of the task force on intelligence that the *American Psychological Association* formed in the wake of the furor over *The Bell Curve*. The agitation among scholars was related to the issue of race and social class, and we should review their materials carefully for they are important variables. Yet, the bottom line, after all the argumentation, was the same as that we wrote long ago, that both genetics and environment must be consider together, for both inevitably interact to determine human behaviors.

A critical perspective on race issues is provided by Nell Painter.[44] As a historian she notes that the idea of a white race has been ignored in history. She traces the development of that idea from early Western civilization so as to show the economic, scientific, and political effects of that concept. She approaches the concept of "race" as an all-too-human invention. The breadth of her study is impressive, and illustrates well the positive and negative reinforcement value of the concept of race. Its value is clear from her discussion of the 'expansion' of "Whiteness". For example, Irish were not considered white at the beginning of the 19th century. She clearly illustrates the ugly side of the mentality of the white European male who thought nothing about selling wifes, parents, siblings, or children for money. Such positions allowed them to have sex with children.

As evidence of the social concern for racial issues, the National Museum of African American History and Culture has now opened in Washington, DC. The journal *Smithsonian*[45] devoted an entire issue to that museum and describes it well. Yet, the overlaps of Outgroups with multiple ethnic groups is true today and global in extent.[46]

CURRENT PROFESSIONAL ASSOCIATIONS' POSITIONS ON RACE

The American Psychological Association[47] has taken a position in opposition to racial discrimination, indicating that such hinders human development. The American Sociological Association adopted a lengthy position statement indicating the need to study the operation of the use of the concept of race and noting that "Respected voices from the fields of human molecular biology and physical anthropology (supported by research from the *Human Genome Project*) assert that the concept of race has no validity in their respective fields"[48]. Other professional associations have taken a similar stand. Thus it is fair to say that contemporary science does not conceptualize "race" as a condition that may be used to evaluate or judge individuals, nor as a physiological determinant, but as a social variable highly deserving of study.

ANTHROPOLOGICAL ISSUES OF RACE

What does Anthropology tell us about "race"? The two profound conclusions of Anthropology about race are (1) it will remain as a concept and (2) it is social in nature. The Human Genome Project[49] indicated that human beings share 99.9% of their DNA . That finding is used as a mainstream argument for rejecting genetics. The Human Genome Project also indicated that about 85% of human genetic variation is within the racial groups, as opposed to between them. It seems reasonable to put the biological variable to rest, and focus on the impact of using the concept of race in terms of the social effects and also for a better understanding of how sociological structures influence outcomes for humans when race plays a role. It is important that we expand the study of race as a categorical variable lending itself easily to groupings of In/Groups and Out/Groups.

SOCIOLOGICAL ISSUES OF RACE

It is a fundamental truism of Sociological thought that behavior is correlated with human beliefs of what is proper and expected as conveyed by the actual and anticipated reaction (such as social rewards and punishments) from the group to which we belong. From early childhood we learn strong prohibitions against some behaviors, and other behaviors are rewarded. A lifetime of social rewards and social punishments for doing or not doing specific behaviors largely (but not completely) determines our chosen life paths. Humans act according to our view of ourselves as well as our concept of other's view of us. What others expect of us not only "causes" our behaviors, but also the way we see ourselves, and that self-view in turn helps determine our behaviors[50]. Social science research can lead to ways that "racial problems", such as deplorable life outcomes for some racial groups, may be alterable in ways that cost less tax dollars, involve simple (but not presently well designed) programs of social change, lead to less victims and improved lives for everyone, including the delinquents headed to adult crime. In what may be one of the more productive research studies with policy implications for turning race issues around, Vargas[51] studied the social structure and peer pressures of adolescent groups. That research showed the impact of peer pressure (commonly recognized as one determinant of delinquency) is manipulatable by other social forces that are presently insignificant in delinquency control programs. Specifically, values of those in power but outside the "delinquent group" may be used to alter lower level group member's behavioral norms. Readers are encouraged to review the Vargas work for both policy planning to reduce racial problems, as well as new research hypotheses.

Terrorism

Currently, we are experiencing a terrorism war impacting all of humanity. A recent analysis[52] reports that from 1970 to 2013 the world experienced 150,000 acts of terrorism. The report, *Peace and Conflict*, is an annual publication of the University of Maryland's Center for International Development and Conflict Management and the Graduate Institute of International and Development Studies. The Global Terrorism Database shows that terrorism has shown a drop, the largest in a decade, going down by 13% for attacks and 14% by deaths. Yet, the statistics involve a 2015 number of more than 28,000 deaths and 35,000 injuries resulted from nearly 12,000 terrorist attacks. The report cautions that we should not assume this is a trend towards ending terrorism, as numbers have gone in "waves" and we do not yet know what lies ahead. There are some parts of the world experiencing substantial increases in terrorism. The report includes substantial papers on biological, chemical, radiological and nuclear threats to humanity, so that our best assumption is that terrorism remains a clear and present global danger and we cannot accurately predict what may lie ahead. It certainly is true that "terrorism" as various forms of evil continues as current and quite visible events.[53] The study does agree with our analysis that group conflicts and the links between hate crimes and terrorism flows logically from the In-Group Out-Group dichotomy we argue is critical to analysis of evil.

How can terrorism be explained? The June, 2016 issue of *Scientific American Mind* includes a special report on terrorism, indicating that domestic terrorism events by Islamic terrorist have recently risen. They are up 38% points since 2011 in France, and 17 percentage points in the USA. That issue reports on the Global Terrorism Index showing a 10-fold increase from 2000 to 2014. Clearly, we face unprecedented evil by type and by number through modern day terrorism.

What causes people, especially youth, to be so attracted to terrorist groups that recruits are willing to give up their lives? Since 2001, Syrian and Iraq terror groups have recruited 30,000 "soldiers" to their cause, and those recruits are not typically psychopaths or mentally ill persons. Rather, it appears they are simply shaped by the sociological forces we discuss in this book. See *The Scientific American Mind,* noted above.

An excellent description of the mechanics of terrorism, war and changes that have recently occurred in how war and terrorism is carried out may be found in the excellent work of Norman Friedman[54]. He describes the war conditions and locations, and includes a discussion of the root causes of terrorism, a topic critical to this manuscript. Comparing terrorism to crime, he argues that if the terrorists are simply evil and predestined to carry out terror acts, it is of little use to consider causes, much as we criminologists would address primary psychopathology. But if it is <u>conditions</u> that cause terrorism, we must understand them. He argues there are two root conditions causing terrorism. The first is the Israeli-Palestinian conflict. The second is the corruption and dictatorship common to Muslim states. Friedman illustrates how the manipulation of those variables at the level of nations is the critical ongoing mechanism. He sees the military strength of the United States to be such that a possible victory over terrorism may be possible. Yet, such a victory would never be complete.

A critical, vital issue for Americans involves our understandable rush to respond and protect our people following terrorist killings, such as the September 11, 2001 appalling, atrocious attack on the USA. The death toll exceeded that of the 1941 attack on Pearl Harbor, for which we went to war. All those deaths were caused by a few Islamist extremists acting on the basis of religious ideas, not unlike the motives behind the Christian crusades in the middle ages. Indeed, both were ignited by religious leaders. Yet, if "evil" is measured by harm to humans, the 911 attack was among the most evil of human events. The 911 Commission Report[55] described our response as "...a nation transformed". The report cites multiple specific and public assaults prior to 9/11 giving clear warning that Islamist terrorists wanted to kill large numbers of Americans. None of our pre 9/11 responses to those earlier events slowed the al Qaeda assault. The Commission Report gives very specific recommendations for what to do and how to do it.

Also, a highly germane report[56], recognizing the 9/11 assault as a "quantum leap in the deadliness and audacity of terror"[57], addresses the conflict between liberty and security brought to the forefront of the American awareness by 9/11. The basic argument of that report is that unchecked governmental power undermines security. They argue that the nature of terror/evil has changed and we may expect to continue to confront truly awful events. They argue:

"...we should focus on perpetrators of crime and those planning violent activities, avoid indulging in guilt by association and ethnic profiling, maintain procedures designed to identify the guilty and exonerate the innocent, insist on legal limits on surveillance authority, bar political spying, apply checks and balances to government powers, and respect basic human rights. Departing from these principles, as the military and intelligence agencies have done, for example, in abusing detainees at Abu Ghraib prison in Iraq, is not only wrong but actually harms national security by fueling anti-American sentiment".[58]

The argument that our government's reaction to terrorist activities must be such as to guard both our lives and our democratic principles is true. Yet, it is not clear from existing research that a cautious approach will not cause innocent American lives to be lost. Clearly, this is an area demanding much public debate and dialogue as well as empirical research quantifying methods of public safety and outcomes. The 9/11 Commission was clear, the terrorist attacks may happen again, and that possibility demands that America attack terrorists and their organizations while at the same time prevent the continued growth of Islamist Terrorism. That Commission recommended a radical reorganization of our defenses and the government.

In modern times the most recognized evil treatment of an "Out-Group" (others unlike us, often to our financial advantage) is the rise of the National Socialist German Workers Party and Adolf Hitler. The impact on those of Jewish faith was and is so profoundly vicious[59] that few of us can grasp the intensity and pervasiveness of its effects. The Nazi "final solution" to the problem of the "International Jew" was intended to totally eradicate the Jewish people from earth. The Nazis succeeded in causing the painful deaths of millions of people simply because they were born Jews. The readers unfamiliar with the impact of the Nazi Party and the disquieting disclosures of this section are urged to read the works of Max Wallace[60]. His work documents the role of greed and evil hate as forces developing and advancing the success of Hitler and the birth of the Third Reich, the Nazi Party, fascism, anti-Semitism, eugenics, the "final solution / holocaust", and links of Americans with those developments. Consider that Henry Ford stated in the _New York World_ that "International financiers are behind all wars ... They are what is called the International Jew: German Jews, French Jews, English Jews, American Jews .... The Jew is the threat"[61]. Henry Ford utilized his involvement with the Nazi Party and directly with Hitler and his close advisors to advance his Ford Motor Company. In the process he influenced the philosophy of Hitler, the path of the war, and support of the Nazi military. This included utilizing "forced labor". He was joined in his impact by Charles Lindbergh. They harmed the Allied war effort, threatened the survival of democratic Europe, and advanced anti-Semitism. Wallace documents that Ford and Lindbergh were not alone in such activities and effects. He reports the involvement of Prescott Bush, the grandfather of President George W. Bush. He notes that Bert Walker (G.W. Bush's maternal great-grandfather) was reported by the US Justice Department as "One of Hitler's most powerful financial supporter in the US"[62]. The Wallace report reveals a complex and presently generally unrecognized involvement of "our" people in humanity's most evil events. Others revered and respected members of "our group" are also reported by Wallace as contributors to evil. His work is verification of the premises of this book.

One of the more vile examples of greed producing evil effects is the action of the Nazi's collaborative effort with the Swiss banking and governmental officials to steal the money of the Jews looted during the Holocaust. The Nazi took everything of value from the Jews, right down to ripping their gold teeth out and melting them down. The Swiss are often portrayed as a neutral and honest banking industry. Indeed, to today people will create accounts in the Swiss banks to avoid taxes and other demands. During the 2nd World War, the Swiss portrayed themselves as neutral and trustworthy, and consequently many who died in the Holocaust had created accounts in the Swiss banks. But the Swiss conspired with Nazi Germany to not only help finance the Nazi war machine, but to disrupt and prevent heirs of the murdered Jews from finding their inheritance. Little had been public regarding that evil operation until Tom Bower[63] produced an expose of the decades long effort to return the vast wealth hidden in the Swiss bank accounts by the Jews to those left alive. The level of obfuscation by government officials in many countries is difficult to grasp. Nazi theft of all things of value owned by Jews in occupied countries amounts to sums yet unknown. The report by Bower concerned not only those funds or the money involved in the industrial collaboration of the Swiss with the Nazi war machine, but also the funds in the Swiss financial institutions, settled as $250 million to be placed in a fund for impoverished Holocaust survivors. Relevant to the present study, those who fought for so long for the heirs of the Holocaust murder victims maintained the issue was not so much the money as truth and morality. This fight was a genuine conflict of good and evil.

The phenomena of Out-Group conceptualization working hand in hand theoretically with greed and power outcomes comes to horrifying reality in the actions of our leaders. Yet, it has not been widely recognized as such. Steven Sora reports a masterful work[64] based in genuine proofs and data. He outlines how western civilization through modern times to today has been lead by those who would "…make today's organized criminals look cherubic." Indeed, the respected leaders of our county and including Founding Fathers as well as today's politicians, will do more than shock the reader. The validity of his argument will make the reader very sad as well as angry.

A frightening analysis of the role of financial greed impacting our government may be found in Bill Bonner's work[65]. He and others have identified the "Deep State", a linking conspiracy to manipulate the financial structure of agencies, regulations, and most important, informal human relationships to the advantage of a few and the disadvantage of the many. His work is resplendent with empirical data and documentation showing the ties of private industry and government. His mesmerizing description of how credit has since the 1970s replaced in several ways the cash of the gold based currency so as to take the world towards a possible collapse will frighten the reader. In 1964 David Wise and Thomas Ross[66] wrote the invisible government "…is a loose, amorphous group of individuals and agencies…" "…that gathers intelligence, conducts espionage and plans and executes secret operations all over the globe." They argued it was new and only recently perceived. Ominously they attest that The Deep State presents a true danger and discuss multiple examples of its operation. Although written shortly after the "invisible government" was begun by President Truman with the National Security Act of 1947, the structure they described remains.

Has humanity evolved beyond the evil we have seen in past events? Regrettably, evil continues, even taking new forms. Consider the attacks on groups of people seen in recent days. The National Threat Assessment Center reports[67] on such events during 2017, including vicious attempts to kill in schools, churches, businesses, and other public sites. Themes of the research included evidence of evil over time and the apparent interpretation of a victim by the aggressors as "Out-Group" members, different from the attacker, such as white supremacy and radical black nationalism. An important aspect of the report is the demonstration of how research on evil can be done is ways leading to control of such events.

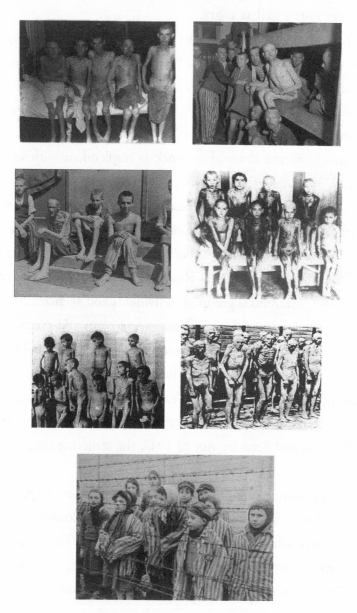

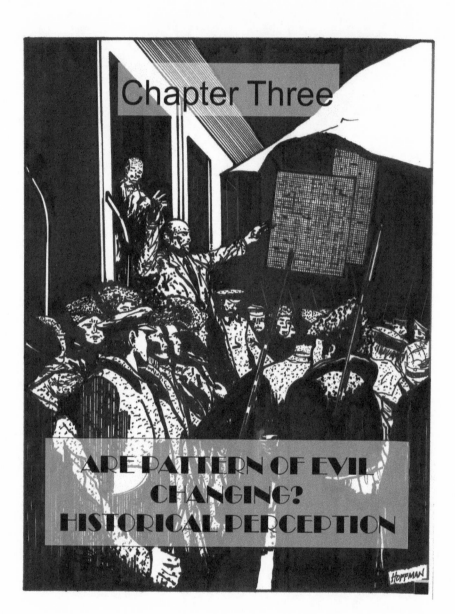

Chapter Three

ARE PATTERN OF EVIL
CHANGING?
HISTORICAL PERCEPTION

HOFFMAN

CHAPTER THREE

Are Patterns Of Evil Changing? – Historical Perception

The invention of the bow and arrow allowed humans to create harm at a distance, rather than physically close to other humans, so that a new type of evil events became possible. In a like manner, the operation of present day technologies presents new evil form possibilities. The songs and music of every culture and religion in the world have been used to define themselves. Love songs are always about the pain or loneliness of relationships, or bad feelings of individuals or groups. We are no exceptions to this rule. Moreover, it should be noted the 7 deadly sins recognized in the Bible all remain today.

God allows human endeavors to go so far and depending on the motive of the person or groups, He does intervene for good. Hollywood had always used the Bible when they need a "Block Buster" money making movie. So, what is the motive when God wants His message sent to the world?

Our Bible, Hymnals and history are full of stories of people or events that will illustrate this. The greatest poem ever written that saved a nation was by an unknown woman; named Julia Ward Howe

(1818-1910). Her husband Samuel Gridley Howe, a wealthy physician, was a member of the Secret Six Abolitionist, worker and organizer of the sanitary commission for the New England troops. Julia was born into an affluent New York family who loved poetry and was asked to write a poem for a literary magazine for five dollars. You must remember the start of the American Civil War was not going well for the Union. In March of 1861 Lincoln was inaugurated. The first crisis was Fort Sumter, but he failed to hold the fort to avoid war. A call for troops was met with mob violence in Baltimore. After federal troops invaded Newport News, Virginia they were forced to withdraw after the battle of Big Bethel, Virginia on June 10, 1861. On July 21, 1861, was the first Battle of Bull Run. The first Manassas battle ended in a rout of McDowell's untrained union forces. Rebels under Sterling Price captured the Union Garrison at Lexington, Missouri on September 20, 1861. The defeated federal troops at Ball's Bluff, Virginia on October 21, 1861 produced dead troops floating down the Potomac River causing panic with the civilian population.

Abraham Lincoln (1809-1865) was losing every political, military, economical, and domestic battle. Into this growing war with all events a little woman, nursing a colicky infant, wrote a poem that saved a nation. You can hear pain and hardships in the words, "I have seen Him in the watch fires of a hundred circling camps in the evening dews and damps; He died to make man holy, let us die to make man free."

Following the Battle at Gettysburg in 1863, the song was sung while the President was in the audience. With tears in his eyes, Lincoln stood and shouted, "Sing it again." The song soon became the unofficial anthem of the Union. "The Battle Hymn of the Republic."

WHITE SUPREMACY MOVEMENT IN THE WORLD

Charlottesville, Virginia in August, 2017 is the first city to feel the full weight of the Neo-Nazi attempt to take control of the streets. This is the same tactic used by Hitler's "brown shirts" in the street of Germany to intimidate the voters and political opposition into submission.

Hitler never had a majority to control the delegates in the Reichstag. He was appointed to chancellor in 1933 and under the control of the Army and Hindenburg; with the death of Hindenberg and support from the Army he controlled Germany.

The history of the third Reich is well known and anti-Semitism still pervades in European life. Remember it was Benito Mussolini who founded the fascist party after World War I in 1922 with the promise of getting the trains to run on time. He was killed by Italian partisans in 1945.

Fascism is still alive in Europe and is operating underground according to Italian Police. Their methods and weapons are very sophisticated.

We don't want any anti-America groups to go underground because of the protections written in our Constitution. We want to know all we can about their ideas or plans.

Back to Charlottesville, Virginia; there were mistakes by both sides-one civilian killed by an auto that strikes a crowd of protestors; two policemen die in a helicopter crash documenting on film the activities for identification and legal proceedings.

Charlottesville was chosen because of the University and the home of Thomas Jefferson who helped write the Declaration of Independence from England. Emancipation Park and the site of Robert E. Lee statue were also involved with slavery in the South. The beginning of slavery started in 1619 in Jamestown and ended in 1865 before the end of the Civil War.

The local police had the thankless job of keeping the opposite sides from escalating into full scale massacre. The white-supremacy group was photographed and systematically tracked and did pay the consequences for their actions. There are many white-supremacy groups; anti-government militias, fascists; militant black nationalists and extremist Islamic groups operating in the United States and the World.

Historical Perspectives

It is the argument of this book that evil is pervasive, that greed is one of the critical determinants of evil (although other causes are also critical), and that we as a society and as scientists have failed to adequately acknowledge the role of social group forces in that process. Indicators and evidence of the validity of this argument confront all of us every day, yet we do not typically act in the collective good but rather for individual reinforcers. Typically, those individual rewards are money or power, and the power typically leads to money. Below we review examples of our argument in the behavior of those to whom we ascribe prestige, power, respect, admiration, and honor. Many other examples can be provided, as the reader will likely agree.

Greed appears in current affairs so often it is taken for granted. Yet, our concern here is to look beyond and below the obvious human behaviors and analyze the development and maintenance of greed and evil. Sometime greed can be harmful to others beyond the perpetrator, yet not be illegal or be questionable. Moreover, greed and evil may be more pervasive and immediate than we realize. As we review below actions by other governments and other than our own leaders, we may feel comfort believing we live in a county where our norms dictate.

We believe we need not fear actions by our leaders. However, this norm is commonly violated, as evidence by politicians and their own financial rewards. Moreover, Belzer and Wayne have recently released a book[68] about controversial cover-ups of what are described as truly awful crimes, and powerful / respected people are involved, as well as organized crime. Comments by Jesse Ventura, as an "afterward" to the book, indicate the incriminating information is proper and patriotism personified. The book outlines the involvement of the government and others in the deaths of Marilyn Monroe, John F. Kennedy, Dr. Martin Luther King, Jr., Robert F. Kennedy, Vincent Foster and others. The work is genuinely frightening. It should be read by all who harbor a sense of complacency and freedom from evil.

Examples:

The Associated Press has followed the increase in the price of drugs as they rose to the point that some who needed them could not afford the drugs. One recent news-story[69] reported a drug company executive "insulting lawmakers" when questioned about "pharmaceutical industry greed" involving the raising of the price of Daraprim about "50-fold". The Gordon and Perrone report indicates there exists a pattern of the pharmaceutical company buying low cost drugs then raising the price dramatically. This is not limited to one company, of course. A survey by the World Economic Forum found that business conflicts at an international level are a primary worry of political leaders globally[70]

A study[71] of misconduct by financial brokers reported one in thirteen brokers had a history of misconduct. One third were found to be recidivists. Such misconduct is most common in countries high in wealthy and elderly people. Garman and also Green argues the Swiss banking system, believed to be a world model of trust, helped the Nazi powers steal from the Jews during WWII.

Attorney Lewis Pitts, after 43 years as a lawyer, demanded his own resignation from the North Carolina Bar on the basis of "...an overall breach by the Bar as a whole of the most basic notions of professional conduct and ethics[72]...". He quoted Alexander Hamilton that the "rich and well born" control the power structure through campaign contributions, while those in the non-rich group suffer substantially in many ways.

The "flagship" university of the State of North Carolina system recently was revealed to have offered courses in the Department of African American Studies that had little or no academic requirements or even attendance rules. Yet, athletes who were selected for such non-courses were given A grades. This allowed the student athletes to use false high grades to continue participation in sports, which was to the financial advantage of UNC-Chapel Hill and the individual athletes. The Chairperson of the Department of African American Studies was fired, but the participation of other faculty and administrators was substantial, and that continues to be investigated. Following the widespread revelation of the academic disgrace, the UNC-Chapel Hill established a new position, a "Chief Integrity Officer". The suggestion of hypocrisy and irony of this new well paid position was noted by citizens.[73]

Citing research from a scientific journal, the People's Pharmacy indicated pharmacy mistakes are shockingly common, in some cases leading to disability or death. The error rate they note is "...more than one in five prescriptions."[74] A personal physician of the author submitted a prescription for a poor and elderly lady. The pharmacist had a question and rather than call the physician, he turned the lady away on a Friday afternoon, leading to a weekend of pain for her. A survey reported in a medical journal[75] indicted that physicians are sometimes dishonest with their patients for fear of being sued. National news reports research[76] from *Johns Hopkins Medicine* that medical errors are the third leading cause of death in the United States, killing almost twice as many people as accidents kill. Deaths by medical error are right behind heart disease and cancer! But, the way statistics are recorded prevent more specific research and keep the problem out of the public eye. The report calls for changes in death certificates and for the Centers for Disease Control and Prevention to immediately add medical errors to its annual list reporting the top causes of death. It estimates that more than 250,000 Americans die each year from medical errors, just behind heart disease and cancer. Medical mistakes that can lead to death range from surgical complications that go unrecognized to mix-ups with the doses or types of medications patients receive, but true and accurate statistics are not available, due to the coding system used by the Centers for Disease Control (CDC). Yet, although medical errors are not well researched, it is likely the public assumes those medical leaders with authority will take action to protect us. *USA Today* reported, "States seldom discipline doctors despite warnings."[77] The isomorphism of the "In-Group" of medical and political failing to protect the "Out-Group" with our theoretical model is obvious. Readers are referred to the investigation report for upsetting details (see footnote 77).

Political events in the interest of the politician at the expense of the public are so common as to be platitudes. Yet, while self-interest is common among most humans, some political events are so harmful / evil as to be genuinely remarkable. An outstanding example is our economic crisis in America. *The Washington Post* reported "…projections show the country's long term fiscal health is in decline, but presidential candidates ignore the problem."[78] The Congressional Budget Office, typically believed to be objective and empirical research based, reported "…our fiscal predicament…is worsening markedly….at the end of 2026 the publicly held federal debt will be 86% of total output."[79]

Bullies are among the most hated of criminals. Some bullies are unlike anything most of us can conceive. One example of this is Albert Fish, not an isolated case. He kidnapped children, killed them and ate them. He was found to be competent to stand trial and executed. Those wishing to know details of individual evil, involving face to face harm, should read the description of his crimes[80]. The descriptions of his evil are beyond detailing here, but we should acknowledge the abstract identification of the various evil acts he committed against helpless children. Schechter lists them as:

1. "Sadism.
2. Masochism.
3. Active and passive flagellation.
4. Castration and self-castration.
5. Exhibitionism.
6. Voyeur acts.
7. Piqueur acts. (Jabbing sharp implements into oneself or other for sexual gratification).
8. Pedophilia.
9. Homosexuality.
10. Fellatio.
11. Cunnilingus.
12. Anilingus (oral stimulation of the anus).
13. Coprophagia (eating feces).
14. Undinism (sexual preoccupation with urine).
15. Fetishism.
16. Cannibalism.
17. Hypererotism (abnormal intensification of the sexual instinct)."[81]

In June of 2016, Omar Marteen, a private security guard, shot over 100 people in the Pulse nightclub of Orlando, Florida[82]. The killing was done with an AR 15 assault rifle and a 9MM semi-automatic handgun. Many of those shot died and the newspapers reported the worse mass shooting in US history. It was reported he killed them because of their sexual orientation. It was also reported the attack was inspired by the Islamic State terrorist group. ISIS sympathizers living as American citizens were noted by the FBI as linked to similar terror acts. Consider also the random killing of 32 students at Virginia Tech, and similar events at Newtown, CT, Las Vegas, NV, Orlando, FL, and Virginia Beach, VA.[83]

Religious Leaders

America was saddened by the recent sex scandal involving Catholic priests, and the Catholic Church hierarchy that covered it for many decades. The level of trust extended to our religious leaders, as well as their assumed personification of morality and ethics, intensified the public response. Moreover, the role of priest involves not only trust and responsibility but also substantial social power and control. The Catholic Church enlisted the John Jay College of Criminal Justice to study this matter and issue a report. That rigorous scientific study, covering the period 1950-2002, found allegations of abuse against 4,392 priests, over 4% of active priests. A total of 10,667 victims of sexual abuse were identified. The financial costs at that time to the Catholic Church exceeded $500,000,000.00. Most victims were males between 11 and 14 years of age. Of known priest offenders at that time, 24% had been referred to the police, 6% were convicted and 2% received a prison sentence. The Pennsylvania clergy abuse report appears to have opened up a vast body of additional concern[84] as part of a world-wide reaction.

We know from our personal experience and from scientific research that our religious leaders are often assumed to be respected and admired as the epitome and embodiment of goodness, proper behavior, and modeling of behavior for all.[85] The Pew Research Center reports survey findings of both Catholic and Non-Catholic as 7 in 10 having favorable opinions of the then current Pope Frances.[86] Yet, the historical assumptions of our religions and our religious leaders is reported in research to be losing ground.[87] A Duke University study found that the percentage of people with "great confidence" in religious leaders declined from 35 percent to less than 25 percent from 1973 to 2008. That study also found that two-thirds of Americans say they would prefer religious leaders to stay out of politics.[88] Yet, even with the shift towards less assumptions of holiness on the part of religious leaders, many have been surprised, perhaps even shocked, by the revelation of John Cornwell's book, "Hitler's Pope".[89] Although there has been common opinion that the Catholic Church did not do enough to speak out against the Nazi holocaust during WWII, Cornwell's work goes much further. With the first outsider access to the Vatican's files on that matter, he states "...nearing the end of my research, I found myself in a state I can only describe as moral shock. ... my research told the story of a bid for unprecedented papal power drawing the Catholic Church into complicity with the darkest forces of the era. I found evidence that from an early stage in his career Pacelli betrayed an undeniable antipathy towards the Jews and that his diplomacy in Germany in the 1930s had resulted in the betrayal of Catholic political association that might have challenged Hitler's regime and thwarted the Final Solution".[90] This includes a collaboration with fascist leaders from 1929 including Mussolini (**Lateran Treaty**), and Hitler (**Reichskonkordat**). A detailed report of these conditions is presented in the work of John Cromwell.[91]

That the moral/ethical/religious leader of the largest body of religious individuals would have contributed to the development, ideas, and very existence of the Holocaust, based on personal professional greed and self-image enhancement is difficulty to believe, but the evidence is presented from sources including Vatican files. That this occurred over so long a period of time and others involved then allowed it is verification of the need for a study such as this book provides. We ask, are none immune from evil and greed? Fortunately, some are immune.

Serial Killers

The attention to serial killers by the media may imply they are a new phenomenon, yet they are not. Consider a Chicago past killer, H.H. Homes, and the selection of the world's worse several killers compiles by Mehrotra. Unusual cruelty, selection of defenseless victims, and eating of their bodies was common.

Dictators

Adolf Hitler

This German Chancellor was legally elected administrator and political leader of Germany. The impact of Hitler is such that he is recognized as the personification of evil. Newsweek noted that "It is vital to our shared experience to understand the rise and reign of the man who inflicted more pain and suffering on humanity than perhaps any other individual in history."[92] In his youth he was not unusual, making good grades in school and considering a career as a Catholic priest. His family structure was not helpful, as his alcoholic father beat him. Yet nothing is apparent to explain a psychopathic development of the worse order. As an adult, he lived in turbulent economic and political times. Indeed, the extreme inflation of German money and the fall of the Weimar Republic set the stage for Hitler's legal appointment as German Chancellor and the legal passing of the "Enabling Act", giving him the power of a dictator. With that power he orchestrated the 1942 Wannsee Conference allowing the legal officials of the government to create the "*final solution*", that is the annihilation of all Jews. He then executed death, cruelty, and suffering on a scale and with a purpose unequaled in history. The German invasion of the Soviet Union caused 25 million deaths. Eleven (11) million Jews and others categorized as "undesirables" such as the disabled died in the holocaust, and millions of others died in other countries. The Newsweek report on Hitler draws parallels between the conditions at the time of Hitler, the political mechanisms he used legally, and the United States of America today. Everyone should read that report, for it strikes home and suggest a present danger. It should be noted that there exist no empirical quantification of the evil the Nazi powers caused, as it is evil beyond description. Of the many books written on this, one stands out to the writers. *Where Was God during the Holocaust*, is a description through the eyes of a prisoner of events in the concentration camps. Those readers with a commitment to understanding evil should read it.

The role of the professional persons, medical, scientific, and other, was an integral part of the Nazi horror. It must be emphasized that this is modern evil, not long ago, although there exist a tendency to avoid recollections. Yet, as this is written the national news[93] is reporting that a former Auschwitz death camp guard has been sentenced to five years in jail after a four month trial, at which many holocaust survivors testified. A Germany court ruled that Reinhold Hanning, 94, an SS guard at Auschwitz from 1942 to 1944, was guilty of being an accessory to the murder of at least 170,000 people. Other similar trials may occur and at least one investigation continues. Recall what the Nazi professional personnel did, beyond ripping skin from the Jews to make lampshades. Baron-Cohen reports of a woman whose hands were cut off and replaced in reverse, as an experiment. Medical schools teach that the best research on human responses to extreme cold was done by Nazi scientists' "immersion experiments" at Dachau, involving Jews in ice water. Garman[94] describes the medical experiments of the Nazi camps as the worse biomedical crimes of modern time, and that the doctors and scientists felt their work was morally proper. The physicists and other natural scientists who cooperated with the Nazi ideology worked on the creation of an atomic bomb. Had they finished that project successfully, we can only speculate what Hitler would have done to the human race. The reports about scientific work on atomic weapons is convoluted and unclear, but it is possible some of the scientists did not work as productively as they were capable of doing, thereby impeding the bomb from finalization. Although the actual events and motivations remain unclear, it appears that although some scientists fully endorsed Nazi ideology, others resisted and a large number were passively resistant[95].

Elie Wiesel was a young boy when he and his family, a respected family of six, were taken by the Nazi SS to a concentration camp. He survived and described his experience as a child inmate in his classic description of the Jews and others in the Holocaust[96] . This harrowing chronicle of what he saw in the death camps (originally titled "And the World Remained Silent") was intended to require humanity to face and recognize evil. We agree, such must be openly confronted. His description of the Nazi interpretation of Jews as so harmful that all should be killed, as less than human, and as impediments to social progress is a must read, despite its horrors. For example, he reported that as a child inmate in the camps he and other children were being marked and "Not far from us, flames were leaping up from a ditch, gigantic flames.[97] They were burning something. A lorry drew up at the pit and delivered its load – little children -- babies!! Yes, I saw it. Saw it with my own eyes…little children in the flames". Others have verified this, and that many babies were alive when thrown into the flames. SS Guards even used babies thrown in the air for target practice.

World War II is reported to have killed 66 million people, of which 20 million were military deaths. One third of all Gypsies were murdered by the Nazis, and eleven million people died in the Nazi death camps. Of Poland's prewar Jewish population, only 10% lived through the war. The horror lingers as the trials of Nazi participants of the concentration camps goes on. SS sergeant Oskar Groening was tried by a German federal court which upheld his conviction for being an accessory to murder at the Auschwitz death camp, his lawyer said Nov. 28, 2016. The history and development of evil through the use of the concentration camps is vividly portrayed, with photographs, by Nikolaus Wachsmann[98] in his coverage of them from the early 1930 through mid 1940s. His work provides extensive documentation as well as vivid portrayal of the unbelievable horror of the camps. Massive in its comprehensive and documented coverage of the development and use of the camps, his work describes evil from the perspective of not only the victims but the Nazi personnel as well, and the description of what the liberators at the end of the war saw and recorded. For the reader focused on the events and description, this work is superb. Our concern in this manuscript is to document and explain so that social scientists addressing criminological issues, and needing to manipulate causes can prevent evil in the future. Few better portrayals of the need for such can be found beyond Wachsmann.

A recent description of the Nazi death camps can be found in the superb work of Lawrence Rees[99], focused on Auschwitz. He portrays the horror of evil Nazi programs in such a way as to mystify the reader. But readers of his work we must be, for the events and our understanding of their cause cannot be allowed to fail and inadequately prevent such evil from reoccurring. His photos, and others as well, are so ghastly and the photos of the prisoners so terrifying, it will be hard to read. But you, the reader of this text, must force yourself to confront what is possible for normal human beings to become. Understanding that we must learn of such unbelievable events as the reports of the Auschwitz crematoriums and the medical experiments by Dr. Mengele, the reader is referred to the eye witness and participant documentation by Dr. Miklos Nyiszli[100], the medical assistant to Dr. Mengele. Be prepared to weep. And you will be startled as you struggle to grasp the magnitude of the evil found in the 15,000 Nazi camps. Sarah Helm[101] presents what for some may be unbelievable descriptions of the experiments on women done in the Nazi camps. Her description and photographs of the cruelty is very difficult to review, but we must in order to grasp the nature of such intentional and extreme treatment of those redefined as other than human. Additionally, the Helm's work portrays the powerful strength of those who survived. Should the Second World War have turned out differently, and had the Nazi powers won, we would have experienced a horror difficult to imagine. The role of "science" would have been used to justify more of the unbelievable human experience we know were carried out for years under the Nazi policies. Scientists operated under the policies of extermination and redefinition of human life that was not "aryan" or white Europeans, primarily Germans, thereby justifying extermination. The experiments in the name of science that utilized human subjects are difficult for many to understand, as they involved measurements of the amount of pain needed to kill, operations without any anesthetic, injecting dye into children's eyes, throwing of living children into crematoriums or open fires, determination of the amount of time naked prisoners would survive in freezing snow, shooting prisoners with poisoned bullets to measure the effects of the poison on death times, placing prisoners in high or low pressure to see when death or exploding bodies occurred were only some of the unbelievable scientific measures.[102] Other scientists worked to develop an atomic explosive device that would have been used on the Allies. In addition to the inhuman distortion of science, the Nazi leaders were also involved with sadistic treatment for its own sake, simply to produce horror and pain in massive amounts. A detailed report of these conditions is presented in the work of John Cornwell.[103] Related in ways that have tantalized historians for years is the impact of the Nazi involvement with occult philosophy. This has become of such interest as to cause *National Geographic* to produce a movie and TV show about Hitler and the occult.[104] These facts and conditions are relevant to our study as they illustrate the abominable dreadfulness that can be caused by "evil", exemplifying the value of this study and the need for the reader to expand the study of evil.

Pertinent to our theoretical argument that membership in groups determines much of human perception of reality is the writing of Heinz Linge, the man who served as Hitler's valet. Discussing the events surrounding Hitler's suicide, and the last meal of Hitler and his aids together, Linge states that Hitler recognized the immediate future would reflect poorly on him but that "…he trusted to the 'later histories' to treat him justly' . They would recognize that he had only wanted the very best for Germany."[105] Linge, as others who served the Nazi cause, acknowledge the death and carnage caused by their actions, yet they often find reason to offer justification and rationalizations, consistent with our position that much that would never be allowed within an "In-Group" is, by often unrecognized allegiance to that In-Group, allowed in the case of Out-Groups. In few instances is this more apparent than in the case of the Nazi terror and specifically the holocaust. And it happened in "today's world" in that many living today were part of it. Only in early 2017 did the last Nuremberg prosecutor, Benjamin Ferencz, die. His observations are consistent with our description of the horror, and of the use of redefinition of people in "Out-Groups". He stated "One of my lead defendants, who killed 90,000, instructed his troops 'If the mother is holding an infant to her breast, shoot the infant because the bullet will go through both of them and you will save ammunition'"[106]. Describing the liberation of the concentration camp he said 'It was if I had peered into hell'. And the defendants were '...educated people; one was a father with five children. They were not all wild beast with horns'". We focus on the role of ingroup/outgroup membership as an empirical variable of critical importance in understanding evil and greed. This emphasis in our formation of theoretical explanation of evil is illustrated and embellished by a scientifically meaningful aspect of the Holocaust: the transmission of evil-effects across generations. The role of a primary "In-Group", the family, plays a central role in that transition, and this buttresses our theoretical focus. The transmission of evil effects through generations has been addressed by several scholars[107] and illustrates for our theory the role and empirical importance of "identity" with "In-Group" membership. In a definitive study of this type, Jacobs reports on the process, the theoretical variables, and the effects of the transmitting the Holocaust experience through generation of family members. Her personal interviews with survivors of the Nazi Holocaust, their children, grandchildren, and great grandchildren revealed that descendent identity was created so as to keep the Holocaust real. She states, "Taken together, narrative, space, ritual, and spirituality constitute the interactive social and cultural framework that characterize the intergenerational transmission of trauma and contributes to the formation of descendant identity."[108] Providing insightful explanations of the operation of our variables of interest, she even discusses at length how "ritual" may be impacted by the location/place it operates. Of high relevance for our theory is her treatment of the differences in outcome when post genocide governments suppress teaching about the past and others allow it. Where In-Group identity maintained conflicts with "Out-Groups" it resulted in higher levels than where government suppressed In-Group/Out-Group conflict. A vital aspect of Jacob's research that is consistent with our ideas involves her recognition that the Holocaust leads to a descendant identity as an in-group that becomes a dominant psychic identity impacting the social psychological aspects of multiple generations.

Herod the Great

Herod was "King" of Judea at the time of Christ's birth. Told by visiting "wise men" that a King of the Jews was about to be or had just been born, he believed such to be a threat to his position. The Bible states "Then Herod, when he saw that he had been outwitted by the wise men, flew into a rage. He gave orders to massacre all the male children in and around Bethlehem who were two years of age and under..."[109]. Klein[110] estimates that the order caused 10,000 babies and small children to be murdered by Roman soldiers.

Genghis Khan

Among other evil acts, he destroyed a major city, killing 700,000 citizens of all ages.

Joseph Stalin

This dictator killed more people than Hitler killed.

Saddam Hussein

As President of Iraq he used chemical weapons against Iran, killing up to 730,000 citizens, and also against the Kurds, killing up to 340,000 people. He carried out other massacres as well.

Mao Zedong (Mao Tse-tung)

This man, Chairman of the Communist Party in China, is reported to be responsible for the biggest mass murder in the history of the world. Dikotter[111], in a recent review of Communist Party files, describes the "Great Leap Forward" as a catastrophe of gargantuan proportions, leading to the deaths of at least 45 million Chinese people. The world outside of China knows little of those events, which included many millions of people tortured to death in an effort to force on the people a new way of life.

There have been other evil men in political positions, using their power to create massive harm. Consider the following political leaders.

Shaka Zulu of Africa, Anastasio Garcia Somoza of Nicaragua, Papa Doc and Baby Doc Duvalier of Haiti, Kim Il Sung of North Korea, Augusto Pinochet of Chile, Nicolae Ceausescu of Romania, Pol Pot of Cambodia, Idi Amin of Uganda, Robert Mugabe of Zimbabwa, Caligula and Nero (both Emperors of Rome), Attila the Hun, Tomas de Torquemada (Inquisitor General of Spain), Ivan the Terrible of Russia, Rasputin of Russia.

Evil Females[112]

Although not selected by gender, the above listings of evil leaders are males. The positions of power and positions of leadership over the years, indeed throughout human history, speaks more to the physiological and strength advantage of males than to any disproportionate ability. Indeed, when presented with the opportunity of power roles, females perform as well as males, and have been as evil as males as well. Consider the limited list of evil females described below.

Dee Casteel

Dee Casteel was the first female in South Florida to be sentenced to death in the electric chair. Appearing to be an average waitress in the International House of Pancakes, she and her lover arranged for the murder of her boss so that after his death she and the lover would share the estate. That such a "normal" woman, well-liked by her friends, would commit murder for profit is the point.

Lizzie Borden

Heard in my early school years was "Lizzie Borden took an ax and gave her mother 40 whacks. When she saw what she had done she gave her father 41". Lizzie Borden, well thought of, was a regular member of a church and appeared to be a respectable lady. Using an ax, she took off both the head of her mother and her father, apparently to get the estate, as the father was planning to change his will. Lizzie Borden maintained that a stranger broke in and cut off their heads. She was found not-guilty, with the possibility that assumptions made by citizens was that a nice lady could not do such an awful, cruel act.

Myra Hindley

Myra Hindley committed, only a few decades ago, the first sex murder of multiple children in modern England. She and her boyfriend would rape, sometimes anally, the children and then kill them. Some of the killings were audio tape recorded and pictures of the children forced into sexual acts were made. Both Myra Hindley and her boyfriend were convicted and sentenced to multiple life sentences.

Karla Homolka

Sex and cruel murders were also used by Karla Homolka. Young girls were the victims, involving anal rape and oral rape, with video recordings of the events as the girls were being ripped apart and killed. She even used those techniques to kill her younger sister.

Rose West

Rose West and her husband sexually abused and cut up their victims, including her daughter. She was convicted of ten murders of the most vicious sort.

Mary Ann Cotton

In the late 1800s, Mary Ann Cotton killed up to 24 people, including her husband and her children. She killed other family members as well. She was convicted and hung.

Elena Ceausescu

Elena Ceausescu and her husband, Romania's President, caused the death of 60,000 people over a period of 24 years, through a "police state" in which she manipulated her husband and others so that they held complete and total power over the citizens. Finally, their draconian[113] suppression and cruel to the death manipulation of the people caused a revolt.

Ilse Koch

Known as the "Bitch of Buchenwald" she and her husband, Nazi SS Colonel Karl Koch, commanded and ruled the Buchenwald concentration camp. While it is difficult to grasp, she and her husband were so cruel they were put on trial by the Nazis themselves and executed. Her victims were the Jews, gypsies, mentally retarded, physically disabled, homosexuals and intellectuals. Known for her sadistic and nymphomaniac behaviors, she would force prisoners to perform perverted sex acts while she watched, then had them tortured, then killed. Her home was decorated with shrunken heads of prisoners and lampshades made from skin ripped from live prisoners. Starting as a young, quite pretty red-head, employed as a librarian, she was seen by Gestapo leader Heinrich Himmler as a wife for Karl Koch, to develop the Aryan race. Her husband was chosen to lead the camp in part because he would use a horsewhip embedded with razor blades to beat prisoners. He also used thumbscrews and branding irons on the prisoners. Under him, the camp worked and harmed prisoners so badly they had no gas chambers as none were needed to kill the prisoners: they died from overwork, starvation and torture. The camp had a special medical research unit, involving castrations without anesthetic, live vivisections, infection of prisoners with fatal diseases for observation, and tests on human resistance to pain, heat, cold, all for Nazi science and protection of the Aryans. Ilse Koch took delight in setting her dog on pregnant women. She organized lesbian orgies with other Nazi women, and had sex with up to a dozen young Nazi officers at a time. She experienced sexual pleasure from other's pain, had prisoners heads cut off and shrunk for display in her home. Also, she had prisoners skinned alive so their skin could be used as leather to make gloves, wallets and lampshades for homes. Even prisoner's hair was used, to make socks. Boiled alive prisoners were made into soap. Finally, the theft of Nazi treasures was discovered and both Ilse Koch and her husband were tried and convicted by a Nazi court. The husband was executed, she was sent to prison and hung herself in her cell. It was noted that she showed no remorse for her crimes, involving 50,000 prisoner[114] deaths.

Natalia Baksheeva

As this is written the newspaper[115] is reporting a Russian couple drugged thirty people over a twenty year period, and skinned them alive. They ate some of the body parts and froze the rest for later meals.

As workers in a military academy, they slipped some human remains into the soldier's food.

Greed

We all have felt we want more of something, so that the psychological propensity to greed is so common in the human race we accept it. Can greed lead to evil behaviors? Yes. And although we typically think of greed as the struggle for money, it involves more than money. One example is the powerful portrayal of behavior of some of our respected and esteemed political and real estate and political leaders. Vicky Ward described some of our respected leaders as they fought over the purchase of real estate. She describes "…lying, cheating, stealing, suing, and tax evasion are just humdrum ways of business. Friendships and alliances get made to be broken; a man's word is never his bond; partners routinely sue one another; wives are discarded and cheated on; but so too are bankers, colleagues and brokers."[116] Evil comes in many packages, and the operation of greed makes clear the absence of goodness.

The Wall Street Journal identifies Morganson's work as an excellent history of the 2008 financial crisis. She reports that the worst economic crisis since the Great Depression began with President Bill Clinton's political push to put an owner in every home. That political move created an unheard of relationship of regulators and lending institutions. She states that "…all the venerable rules governing the relationship between borrower and lender went out the window, starting with the elimination of the requirements that a borrower put down a substantial amount of cash for a property, verify his income, and demonstrate an ability to service his debts"[117]. She indicates that these events were based on greed, corporate corruption and government support, involving the highest levels of government and corporate leadership. The Federal Reserve devoted ***$8 trillion dollars*** to bailing out the institutions. The role of power associated with high office and wealth becomes apparent, as Morganson lists many important officials who benefited greatly, were responsible, but were not charged. The impact was international, involving"…trillions of dollars in investments lost around the world, millions of Americans jettisoned from their homes, and fourteen million U.S. workers without jobs". (page xiv) … after the trillion dollar bailout began, congress and the administration officials did little to repair the damaged system and insure such a travesty could not happen again" (page 7). What was the reckless endangerment of the entire nation? It was greed and self-interest as we address in this book. Moreover, Morgenson makes clear the rich and powerful were <u>NOT</u> held accountable. Not only does she make clear that responsible leaders were not held accountable or charged, but that they have advanced professionally and continue to hold high positions since the debacle. She identified, among many others, as examples well suited for this book, a Treasury Secretary, a National Security Advisor to the US President, a Deputy Secretary of State for management and resources, and many others including leaders of financial institutions.

Yet another highly respected and credible analyst of contemporary greed is Lou Dobbs[118]. His book, published in 2004, begins with a statement germane to our topics: "Never have there been fewer business leaders willing to commit to the national interest over selfish interest, to the good of the country over that of the companies they lead."[119] Dobbs is one of a very few social/political commentators broadly respected from multiple political perspectives. His book was written from an extended frustration over outsourcing of jobs and resources, erroneously termed "free trade" by many. He saw that such selfish outsourcing eroded the American social structure and values. He not only makes the argument that greed in the public and private sectors may cause the end of our republic, but also gives the facts and figures to back up his arguments.

Moreover, he gives the names of the individuals involved!! His work is presented in a easily readable fashion, but the issues are complex. Fundamental to the issues are the following documented patterns.

1. Public and private jobs are transferred to foreign labor markets for cheaper costs. Multinational corporations and the political structure collaborate to one another's interest, rather than the interest of the American people, who suffer because of that collaboration. He notes that corporations spend more on lobbying than the federal government pays for its staff.[120]

2. Multinational corporations move money to and from sources outside America in order to avoid paying legitimate taxes. Dobbs explains how this is done.[121] He identifies the cause as "greed".

Dobbs identifies 12 "myths" of outsourcing and free trade that have been used by politicians and corporation executives to justify the clearly counterproductive arrangements identified above. They are counterproductive for the American people and highly beneficial politically and financially for America's leaders. We have been transformed into the largest debtor nation is the history of the world. Dobbs has an answer[122]. Yet, the current political arena does not show great evidence we are headed in the non-greed direction that Dobbs proposes. Recall the impact of much of the evil we have discussed has been on individual victims. Not so the impact of forces that change a financial structure.

Another TV commentator who became concerned with the financial situation in America is Charles Gasparino of CNBC. The title of his book tells us much about his analysis: **"The SELLOUT – How Three Decades of Wall Street Greed and Government Mismanagement Destroyed the Global Financial System"**[123]. His book begins with a listing of individuals and firms to whom he ascribes the fault for the financial failure. It continues as if it is an exciting novel, and it has both good and bad actors, but it is real and frightening. Gasparino describes the same variables that Dobbs (above) described, primarily "greed" involving both power and money.

In 2011 Madrick published an exceptionally comprehensive analysis of the financial crisis[124]. Covering multiple individuals in multiple roles, he concludes we do not yet know if the actions that were taken will prevent a reoccurrence of the greed based debacle. Yet, despite the evil described he finds some good people and good events in the history of the financial mess. He write "Nevertheless, TARP, the fiscal stimulus, and the Federal Reserve's aggressive loans and guarantees, known as quantitative easing, it should be reemphasized, did stop the collapse and shorten the recession. The Keynesian response did work. By 2009 Wall Street was back and operating, and the recession was declared ended by the summer of that year."[125] Yet, the book identified awful and evil effects, and warns "Washington has not come forward with a well-developed plan for long term growth and a reoriented financial industry that would do what is it supposed to do – channel savings to productive uses".[126]

Vennard[127] reported in 1964 a clearly upsetting, indeed provocative and fear-provoking indictment of the role of greed for both power and money as leading to the downfall of America. He cites names and events leading to the destruction of the U.S.A. in ways difficult to describe. As he predicted the national debt has risen and as 2017 is shown below[128].

current	Debt Held by the Public	Intragovernmental Holdings	Total Public Debt Outstanding
03/01/2017	$14,408,362,699,940.62	$5,512,056,071,348.65	$19,920,418,771,289.27

The Federal Reserve Act of 1913, which set up the central banking system of the US, is seen by Vennard as a primary mechanism for the manipulation of monetary matters to the advantage of unscrupulous financiers. The document he wrote, *"50 Years of Treason in 100 Acts"* covers many variables but includes evil and greed. He sees evil and greed as leading to the end of the USA.

Pharmaceutical Companies and practicing physicians

Do we not unreservedly trust our physicians to act in our interest, as their patients? Are we not taught in high school the physicians in medical school take an oath to "do no harm"? As their colleagues are the drug companies who research and sell the compounds to make us well, do we not by implication trust that entire professional group? An argument can be made that such was the case in the past and it may be changing. One superb research study of what is described as the "...dark side of American medicine" is Melody Petersen's report setting forth in convincing empirical detail how the drug companies became marketing machines causing many of us to become addicted to prescription drugs. Of course, the compliance of the practicing family physician is necessary and indeed, she sets forth evidence that the "encouragement" by the drug companies for the physicians to prescribe the company's drugs is causing substantial harm. She indicates that in 2005 the US patients spent $250 billion on prescriptions, or twice as much as on higher education or automobiles. This is true despite the fact such drugs are one of the leading causes of death. The profit seems related to her argument that only 10% of the price paid for the drugs by you and I, goes to pay for the raw material and manufacture! And, she cites the drug companies as spending more for lobbying in the US government than any other industry. The reader of this manuscript is strongly encouraged to read the Petersen report[129], even though it will make you sick.

PART TWO
CAUSES

Chapter Four

THEOLOGY AND EVIL

CHAPTER FOUR

Theology and Evil

Religion has played the primary role in the definition of good and evil. It even relates them to legal issues, as a lawyer was identified as the professional trying to put Jesus on the defensive by asking him to define goodness. The Bible[130] states the attorney asked "…which is the greatest commandment" and Jesus replied "You shall love the Lord your God with all your heart, with all your soul and with all your mind…. And the second is like it: You shall love your neighbor as yourself". One element of God's word here is the implication that to love God is to adopt the values and norms set forth by God. And "loving your neighbor" is to resist the effects of other/ group hostility. This is, in effect, affirmation by Jesus of the value of our conceptualization of groups and their impact on evil.

The definitive book on this chapter is of course the Bible. Also, the link between evil, our topic, and intelligence/consciousness beyond the physical world is addressed well by Garman.[131] He notes that God, a supernatural being, has a purpose humans cannot understand, and it is that purpose based in the totality of love for humankind, that Garman uses to answer his question "Where was God during the holocaust?" He notes that God, in the form of his son Jesus, suffered as did the Jews at the hands of the Nazis. He concludes that suffering for reasons known to God but beyond our reasoning is part of the overall Divine Plan. The level of suffering of Jesus at the hands of the Roman executions and torturers has been described by medical scholars today.[132]

The most enduring questions throughout human history have included *Does God Exist?*[133] *Why does He allow Greed and Evil? – Does the Devil Exist? What does the Devil Cause?* This chapter will address those and other profound questions, but unlike chapters resting on research and science we offer no definitive answers, other than a review of issues and beliefs. The authors are Christians and this chapter will focus on the interplay of the variable/concept "evil" in Christian theology.

Symbiotic Relationship of Good and Evil

In this monograph we review some examples of "goodness" so as to buttress our claim that both good and evil are concrete forces that merit scientific study. It may be seen from our examples above that religion in several forms, denominations, and ideologies have played and continue to play a critical, indeed fundamental, role in both variables. In this section we discuss elements of the Christian religion involved with the concept of evil. The Christian religion has utilized the concept of "sin" as largely but not exclusively synonymous with our variable of "evil". There are some human events / behaviors that we consider "evil" as a scientific variable, but are not always conceptualized by Christianity as "sin". For example, some political acts such as withholding a vote on a bill so that the political system is disrupted may be seen as evil but not sinful. The logical dilemma of having only one opportunity to act and faced with killing one person and saving many, but not both, and the one person is your friend, involves killing (evil) but saving many people (good).

Our review of the Christian Doctrine concerned with "sin" or "evil" literature found that the historical extent of involvement of evil with doctrine, the complexity of the issue, the theoretical Christian relevance of our review, reveals unrivaled difficulties in the use of the concepts as scientific variables. Indeed, given the premise that a supernatural God created them, there will remain an unreachable component. Thus, for the reader concerned with the issue of "theology and evil" beyond our treatment, we encourage a review of the citations we have provided[134] as well as our work.

Evil plays an essential role in human behavior and spirituality, yet is not widely discussed in Christian writings. For example, Collins[135], in a lengthy tome, reviews the entire Bible, event by event, yet devotes only one (1) reference to "evil" and discusses it on only two pages. There, and typically found in theological literature, evil is presented and operationalized as Satan in a struggle with good, or God. Evil is defeated by God and remains under God's control.[136]

The involvement of evil in Christian theology rest in large measure on the concepts of human nature and sin, resolved by way of God's grace, or in human affairs, forgiveness or salvation. The relationship of man and woman with God as similar entities, that is, similar images or with parallel / analogous features, apart and unlike aspects of other living organisms, is critical. Thus sin, associated only with man and woman, arises from the choice to abuse free will. The original conflict of humanity illustrates that God early recognized sins of lust and greed. Premises to such a relationship includes the reality of free will, although the early misuse of it in human affairs leads to compromised free will. Thus, sin is seen as similar to a hereditary illness that cannot be cured by the sick person, only by God.

Carus[137] argues "The question as to the nature of evil is by far the most important problem for philosophical, religious and moral considerations... it is sin that imparts worth to virtue". His astoundingly thorough coverage of the history of the devil addresses the relationship of God and the devil, noting that the struggle of the two has existed throughout history. His coverage of human actions documents and demonstrates that arrangement, as do his illustrations. His hundreds of illustrations of the devil from multiple cultures and times portrays an excellent review of the many ways humans have seen God and the devil, that is, good and evil. As do others we cite, Carus argues humanity is evolving to a new scientific objectivity. Good and evil will be operationalized as components of a real essence, an objective authority through which right and wrong, good and evil, converge. The contrast of evil to good will reveal both. Having presented the positive value of good and evil actually existing side by side so as to allow for positive events to result, Carus describes evil as quoted below.

"Satan may be the representative of rebellion; God represents liberty. Satan may promise independence by a call to arms against rules and order; God give independence by self-control and discretion. Satan is sham freedom; in God we find true freedom. Satan is an indispensable phase in the manifestation of God; he is the protest against God's dispensation as a joke and an imposition, and thus revolting against the law prepares the way to the covenant of love and spontaneous good-will"[138]

"He is hatred, destruction and annihilation incarnate, and as such he is the adversary of existence, of the Creator, of God."[139] (page 482.)

Multiple Reports of Love and Good

Far too many books have been written about love and goodness for us to attempt anything resembling a review of the literature. Yet we can cite some that illustrate that documentation of "good" far outweighs reports of "evil". We believe that goodness will prevail over evilness and that the existence of evil, awful though it may be, can and does serve a purpose.

Consider the work of Bell in his book "Love Wins".[140] He reviews multiple examples of love and goodness and merits review by our readers, perhaps to balance our discussion of evil. This chapter provides an opportunity to recognize the antithesis of evil, that of goodness and constructive virtue. God's love, bravery, and self-sacrifice appear throughout history. It is beyond the boundaries of this book to attempt a weighting and comparison of good and evil, but we must recall the good humankind has shown. Below are some examples, limited although they may be.

The Churchill Club

The Nazi forces, described above, occupied Denmark from 1940-1945, and the Danes did much to resist them. Yet the initial reaction to the Nazi invasion was weak. Resistance began to grow strong from the efforts of several young boys, in the 9th grade, who formed a group to resist. Their fight against the German occupying force is described in a spellbinding book, recommended to all readers.[141]

The Good News Network

This internet source reports good news of kindness (see https://www.goodnewsnetwork.org)

Corrie ten Boom

The Nazi holocaust, perhaps the most evil event of all time, provides an opportunity for beautiful and virtuous things that could not have happened without it. Many example exist. One of substantial impact was that of the life of Corrie ten Boom, a Dutch Christian who helped many Jews escape the Nazi Holocaust during World War II. She hid them in her closet, the Nazi officials learned of it and she was locked up. Much has been written about her experiences as a brief search on the internet will show. Another well-known opponent of the Nazi party was theologian Dietrich Bonhoeffer. A review of their work will provide clear evidence of the existence of good and the role of evil in making good a possibility.[142]

Who was Uncle Tom?

A major Catalyst for the civil war was the book 'Uncle Tom's Cabin', or 'Life Among the Lonely', written by Harriet Beecher Stowe (1811-1896). In March 1852, she published her book. Within five years, it was the biggest success in American publishing history with five hundred thousand copies sold. It was translated into twenty languages. Harriet Beecher Stowe was an educated woman, mother, writer, and fervent abolitionist who met Abraham Lincoln at the White House and was surprised when Lincoln said: "So you're the little woman who wrote the book that started this Great War?" During the 1850's and even up to 1861, peace was still possible but the book removed the issue from dry political talk to a more hardened line between anti-slavery and slaveholders.

The real Uncle Tom was based on the life of Josiah Henson, a Maryland slave who desired a better life. He was a born leader of his people and was responsible for running the plantation for his master. He was so successful that he earned money for his increasing output of the workers which aided in their well-being.

Henson tried to work within the system to free his wife and children and was betrayed every time by workers or overseers. He educated himself so he could become a minister and spokesperson for his people. He was trusted by owners and allowed to move freely amongst his people. After many hardships and contacts he was able to escape to Canada with the help of the 'Underground Railroad.' Once in Canada, he became a successful Methodist preacher and foreman. He helped other former slaves to read, write, and learn a trade. He never returned to the United States.

The American Civil War was unlike any other civil war in the world. The people especially the leaders, spoke the same language, shared the same religion, schooling, political beliefs, and economics. In the 1860 census there were more millionaires in Mississippi than any other state at that time. The South was adamant about States rights with the states free to leave the Union and form a Confederacy. The North was adamant about preserving the Union, but even Lincoln had trouble holding Northern states together (Northwest territories: MI, WI, MN, IA) and New York City, a free trade zone for economic reasons.

There are many reasons the South lost the war, but without help or recognition building, a new nation is impossible. The only time the south had a chance for foreign recognition or support was between October 1861 to December 1862 with Robert E. Lee (1807-1870) and Thomas J. Jackson (1824-1863). Both men were a team with good defensive-offense exploiting opportunities wherever or whenever possible. Albert Sidney Johnston (1803-1864) and Patrick Cleburne (1828-1864) in the Western operations were good like-minded men with defensive-offense.

The North suffered with leadership at the top. Lincoln (1809-1865) was no military thinker. He had to learn from experience or on the job training. Yet, Lincoln was the consummate politician who was able to work with the people. His wisdom in handling these for the good of the Union, despite a cabinet rent with jealousy and hatred made a stronger Union. Lincoln did have one of the best militaries planner in the whole army, Winfield Scott (1786-1866), who proved to be sound. Both Virginians, he even recommend Robert E. Lee as commander of the Union Army. Lincoln never gave up and he finally, after many failures, found Ulysses Simpson Grant (1822-1885). Lincoln and Grant succeeded in defeating "Bobby Lee's' Armies" and set a policy of reconciliation in motion that was the envy of the world.

Lincoln was assassinated on April 14, 1865 by John Wilkes Booth at Ford's Theater. Andrew Johnson became the 17th President of the United States. Resolved to follow Lincoln's plans for reconstruction without bitterness or malice, Johnson clashed with radical Republicans in congress. His administration was one of constant political abstractions and almost ended with impeachment against him, which failed by one vote.

Reconstruction failed to bring the south into the Union by peaceful means and by the 50th anniversary of the Civil War 'Jim Crow' Laws were passed and operated in full force. With the 100th anniversary, two world wars had began to change the image of American ideals. Co-author Hoffman and his family witnessed the reenactment of the first major battle of the Civil War on a hot summer day at Manassas, Virginia. The sight of the battle on a scale of 1861 and sequential of events in following battles created appreciation of the sacrifice others made for their beliefs.

The co-authors lived through the Civil Rights movement in the army, putting soldiers in a strange twilight zone. With riot control training and helping maintain law and order, it was more than they bargained for. In our travels and duties overseas with the military, co-author Hoffman has seen families sell their children as slaves to keep the family with the necessities of life. Kidnapping in most of the Third World countries is still a 'Cottage Industry' with whole villages involved; so slavery is still alive and doing well!

The Union has withstood revolution, Civil War, two World Wars, police actions, and war on international terrorism and still looks forward to a better future. Remember, in all of this our nation found time to go to the moon and back.

When co-author Hoffman was stationed in Japan he visited many historical places, such as Kyoto and Nara, ancient Japanese cities which are used as backgrounds for all the Samurai movies. The people in those cities showed much reverence to fallen warriors. The natives were dressed in all period dress; the women in colorful dress of ancient Japan. In the 1860's Emperor Meiji decided to modernize Japan and eliminate Samurai warriors. The American movie, 'The Last Samurai" depicts that Civil War in graphic details. It was brutal to say the least. Every man was killed outright and the women and children were used to the benefit of the victors.

The devil

Our investigation of evil and greed would be impotent without mention of the ultimate source of wickedness, Satan. The Christian Bible provides a vivid portrayal of his creation by our God. Academic works have described him.[143] The Church of Satan has a website[144] although the true nature of the groups representing themselves as the officials of Satan remains unclear. Perhaps the best portrayal of the nature of satanic followers, the satanic "philosophy" and the satanic church is the Satanic Bible.[145] It includes a description of the Black Mass, sufficiently offensive and pornographic as not to be quoted here. Yet, the *"Satanic Statements"* give a powerful description of the evil and immorality they attempt to achieve. Those statements follow:

1. Satan represents indulgence, instead of abstinence!

2. Satan represents vital existence, instead of spiritual pipe dreams!

3. Satan represents undefiled wisdom, instead of hypocritical self-deceit!

4. Satan represents kindness to those who deserve it, instead of love wasted on ingrates!

5. Satan represents vengeance, instead of turning the other cheek!

6. Satan represents responsibility to the responsible, instead of concern for psychic vampires!

7. Satan represents man as just another animal, sometimes better, more often worse than those that walk on all-fours, who, because of his "divine spiritual and intellectual development," has become the most vicious animal of all!!

8. Satan represents all of the so-called sins, as they all lead to physical, mental, or emotional gratification!

9. Satan has been the best friend the church has ever had, as he has kept it in business all these years!"[146]

The Satanic Bible is unlike other philosophical works, of a religious or ethical nature, for it is a collection of hedonistic and self-indulgent paths to debauchery. The reader is not encouraged to review it other than for purely academic reasons. Yet, acceptance of the existence of one supernatural entity, our Christian God, leaves the door open for the logical existence of others. Carus[147] argues "...and if we have to declare that the idea of God is a symbol signifying an actual presence in the world of facts, should we not expect that the idea of the devil also represents a reality?" These are profound issues and should be pursued by our philosophers with an analytical interest in evil. Such work is needed as the ideas have extended themselves into the realm of fear and civil discourse, as illustrated by the Church of the Flying Spaghetti Monster[148]

A respected scholar, author and psychiatrist has reported[149] personal interactions with the devil. That weighty review of evil directly experienced concludes with an acceptance of the need to change science so as to include it. He states "But the acceptance of demonology into the scientific fold is not going to happen -- at least not until history itself is reformed, not until a 350 year old separation of the world of supposed natural phenomena from the assumed world of supernatural phenomena is revisited, and recognized by all concerned as having been a gigantic mistake."[150]

The Role of Evil in Christian Theology and Science

The part played by evil as a concept in theology and in science are intertwined. Despite the complexity of the issues, they must be addressed as science should be encouraged to address more about evil in all its forms. Yet materialistic science, which has reigned in recent times, continues to express difficulty with utilizing measures that cannot be physically operationalized. One of the more complete coverages of this intrinsically challenging interplay of concepts is the work of Lindberg and Numbers.[151] They provide a readable historical treatment of the development of religious and secular ideas as they intersect, an extremely complex task at best. They show that in recent times naturalistic science addressed present and reproducible phenomena, issues that can be measured without evoking supernatural variables. Religion addressed the supernatural and questions of original creation,

God, Satan, and miracles. In the mid-1980s a movement by theistic scientists and others began to reexamine the assumptions underlying the separation of the two modes of thought. That movement, known as "Intelligent Design", includes the argument that to reject concepts because they do not fit your philosophy is not consistent with the scientific method, so that naturalistic-only scientists are illogical and irrational. It appears the division of philosophical positions is shifting, so that there are now substantial numbers of both citizens and scientists on both sides of the argument.[152]

As an example of this logical conflict, consider a recent development of scientists investigating "near death experiences." That has produced what many naturalistic scientists have found to be remarkable, and for some, unacceptable conclusions. A near-death experience (NDE) involves conditions reported by persons who are close to death or who are in a situation of physical or emotional crisis. The International Association of Near Death Studies[153] reports that between 4 and 5 percent of the general population have had an NDE. In the U.S., that comes to about 1.5 million people. Although as a focus of scientific inquiry this research is new, a considerable number of research studies have been done, and many credible, prior naturalistic scientists are in agreement regarding conclusions. They indicate that the research shows consciousness separates from the physical body and operates independent of it during the NDE. Hard empirical evidence is presented that suggests that a person's consciousness is an objective, autonomous entity within reality. Although the traditional explanation of consciousness is that it is produced by the brain's activity, scientists and scientific associations argue an equally valid interpretation is that the person's "mind" or "soul" or "spirit" interfaces with the brain to produce consciousness. The argument is made that the evidence is so strong, empirically, that the traditional model of consciousness must be abandoned as it no longer fits the evidence. This research opens avenues for the consideration and study of evil that will be groundbreaking and innovative.

Scientific materialism[154] maintains that only physical reality, as observable by science, is all that exists. There is nothing beyond the limits of that measurable reality. Contrary to that position is that of the research cited above that consciousness extends beyond our brains so that non physical reality, such as God, does exist. If such a realm exist, then it is logical to investigate the existence of the devil and of evil.

CREATION THEORIES

Why there is something rather than nothing is an ancient as well as a contemporary question. Multiple explanations exist to explain the universe. One well accepted (but not by all) idea is called the "Big Bang". Scientists have found that all parts of the universe are flying away from one another so that in the past they must have been closer together. Thus, everything at one point in the past was only one very tiny spot. Then it exploded to create all time, space, matter, and energy. That was about 14 billion years ago. Prior to that there was nothing, not even the tiny spot. There was no time, space, matter, or energy. If those scientists are correct, as they in our opinion are, what was there when there was nothing? We accept as a scientific truism that if something exist and was caused / started, then the cause was other than the something. Thus, the reasonableness of the existence of God may be seen. There are so many arguments about a personal God it is beyond our capacity to review all of them. And our concern is with evil and greed, a limited part of theology. Below we review, in a limited fashion, aspects of Christian theology to help us understand the Creator of everything. Also, we should also note the multiple explanation of the universe other than the Big Bang theory. For example, the Big Bounce theory argues the universe is cyclic. That means that our current universe was formed after the collapse of a previous universe, and that these cosmological events are repeated infinitely. As is true of many of the theories, logical fallacies present themselves. It is asked what started the series of universes as they cannot logically extend backward indefinitely. Consider the arguments below.

OMNIPOTENCE

If God is to play a role in a premise of causes of good and evil, we must recognize He / She can do anything. Some have argued that logically God cannot exist if He / She cannot do something, a condition that occurs once He/She creates the universe. But self-limitation can be reversed. So He / She is omnipotent. Consistent with these premises is the argument below of how evil fits into a good God's actions.[155]

1. *Everything that exist was created by God.*
2. *Everything was created good by a good God.*
3. *Evil is not real but is a "lack of goodness".*
4. *Thus, evil does not come from God but from human's use of God given free will.*

Yet, the presence of evil and suffering continue to be a theoretical problem. One logical impediment is that some events which seem to be evil may lead to a greater good. Garman's work, and that of Kushner, are profound illustrations of such effects / outcomes.[156] Fundamental to the issue of a good God and human suffering / evil is <u>human free will.</u> Evil has long been thought to originate from "original sin". The first human, or perhaps early humans, developed a propensity to act in his/her own interest rather than in the interest of another, perhaps necessary for survival. Any such learned behavior was passed along from the original evil. We argue such transmission is consistent with our theoretical conceptualization and use of psychological learning theory. Thus, the authority/control by the Creator and human free will fit our theoretical framework.

Finally, we agree many, perhaps all, the issues of original evil, including passing it along through generations, and the reasonableness of both a Creator and evil are well addressed by current theory called "Intelligent Design". Basically, that theory finds an "irreducible complexity" to the universe that requires an intelligent creator.[157] Finally, we note Christianity, about 1/3 of humanity[158] acknowledges that Jesus Christ was killed and resurrected. Given this as a premise it follows the Creator came to humanity and thus supports the theology of a Creator and evil.

Multiple Reports of Hate and Evil

Human Sacrifice

Of all the forms of evil we have discussed the killing of babies in very painful ways to secure favor of a supernatural being (a "god"), cutting apart young children for the sale of their body parts, and the effort to extend the horror, pain and fear the victims experience are but example of this widespread and continuing practice. Shreeve's study of this profoundly disturbing type of evil remains one of the academically best reports available. He begins with brief illustrations, as follows:

"New York, USA, 2000. Newborn baby girl with umbilical clamps still attached found floating in a jar of formaldehyde... London, England, 2001. Headless and dismembered body of a 5 to 7 year old boy found in the Thames.... Bochum, Germany, 2002.... Bride of

Satan....hacked a friend to death and drank his blood.... Lima, Peru, 2004. Decapitated baby boy...."[159]

Those of you reading Shreeve's work will likely put it aside often as the description of suffering creates anguish in the reader. His conclusion about the causes of human sacrifice indicates it is caused not by reasoning or greed, but by superstition or belief. Moreover, he argues humans have two personalities, each governed by a different part of the brain, either the left or right side. Others have hypothesized innovative causative variables and suggested we are on the verge of a shift in our overall scientific model from a materialistic one to another model. Certainly, Shreeve has suggested an evolving theoretical explanation / model of evil is likely to be forthcoming in science.

A critical aspect of his work involves his discussion of Satanism, both the "Church of Satan" (or "libertarianism") and the Satanists actually following Satan as lord of all evil. The former are intellectuals but the latter carry out quite distinctive evil acts. The argument Shreeve puts forth that humans have two distinct personalities, governed by the different part of the brain, allows some to operate as a Satanist, cutting open the stomachs of babies and pulling out their eyeballs as sacrifice, and otherwise behaving normally. His work ends with a prediction the horror will continue.

We have focused on "evil and greed", defining the terms earlier in detail (see Chapter 3). We have agreed that "evil" is any intentional human action causing or being capable of causing "pain" in others. "Pain" we define as any type of injury, harm, distress or suffering. These "outcomes" involve a process, an intent, a cause, and a result. "Greed" we see as a primary, **but not exclusive** cause of evil. Our efforts to define these variables as both abstract and operational concepts is prompted by a lack of emphasis in scientific fields and research on limited types and categories of evil. It is argued that scientists have paid little attention to the broad concept of "evil" and more attention to the observation of "good". Yet in the scientific literature "good" has received less scientific attention than is desirable. It is clear that one scientific effort stands out as atypical (but highly appreciated scientific rigorous research). Indeed, for those concerned with the obverse of our topic should go first to the work of Stephen Post and his fellow scientists.[160] They have executed a fundamental principle of science, a review of previous scientific work on the topic of interest. The work was generated by an identical condition to that prompting our study of evil: a belief the present scientific concepts of love were inadequate. Defining love as "...a creative linguistic transposition of agape, the ancient Greek word for love of all people that is associated with God's exception-less love for humanity: the essence of love is to effectively affirm and to gratefully delight in the well-being of others..."[161] They include the additional concept of "altruism" in their annotated bibliography.

Consistent with our interpretation of the condition of scientific assessments of critical variables, they argue "Some would argue that the ills of contemporary life are largely traceable to a deficiency of altruistic behavior. Greed and the self-seeking nature of a consumer culture are considered responsible for the deterioration of social bonds that once kept life more humane".[162] After their genuinely impressive review of the scientific literature they note the research found is "woefully underdeveloped". We agree and recommend their book for all readers. Their review covered the major databases in philosophy, political science, religious studies, sociology, urban studies and a broad-based data foundation. Not only do we believe their work to be unique and powerful support for our premises, but they complement our work so as to fit into what they described as an "emerging discipline". Coupled with the works we cite on new approaches to human consciousness, it is indeed a new discipline.

Chapter Five

SOCIAL, GENETIC AND PSYCHOLOGICAL CAUSES OF EVIL AND GREED; SCIENTIFIC METHODS REJECT NO HYPOTHESIS!

Four horseman of the Apocalypse

CHAPTER FIVE

Social, Genetic and Psychological Causes of Evil and Greed; Scientific Methods Reject No Hypothesis!

So as to prepare oneself for explanation, and dealing further with the complex issue of how we define and describe evil and greed, the student of evil may wish to review journalistic and literary elaborations. For one excellent discussion about evil and its elaborations / manifestations, see the work of Lance Morrow[163], a TIME magazine essayist. His work, not empirical science but rather logical and insightful thoughts, includes a chapter "Why Do They Do It?", and he specifies the following.

- o *"Because it gives them pleasure.*
- o *Because it gives them power.*
- o *Because they don't know any better.*
- o *Because they are afraid of their victims.*
- o *Because they think that the evil they are doing is righteous, or good, or necessary.*
- o *Because they are indifferent to the suffering of others.*

o   *Because they are too morally stupid to recognize the evil they are doing.*

o   *Because they are forced to do it by people holding power over them.*

o   *Because they are caught in a mob's frenzy.*

o   *Because they feel a perverse itch to do harm and it occurs them that they may do so.*

o   *Because it is customary among their people and not to do it would be a breach of community tradition or ceremony.*

o   *Because it is an accident.*

o   *Because they are habituated to it.*

o   *Because they suffer from a compulsion*

o   *Because they themselves were treated evilly once.*

o   *Because Satan makes them do it."*[164]

Although Morrow clearly has substantial exposure to and grasp of evil, he concludes it is not possible to understand evil.

In this chapter we review many theoretical and empirical attempts to explain evil and to measure it. The "scientific method" accepted today is the paradigm best used to specify evil as a scientific concept and to quantify it, including its effects and outcomes. Clearly evil and greed are not quantifiable so as to allow for elements, components and causes to be described in measurable terms as we measure height of a building or the number of persons in a room might be measured. Nevertheless we must attempt to understand and describe such concepts as aspects of our world using the same methods as used to compare the gas mileage of two different models of cars. Such systematic procedures are ancient, from the times of Aristotle who used what we now call the inductive argument later expanded by Francis Bacon. That scientific method in its elaborations is fundamental to all of empirical scientific inquiry today. The power of that method, especially for those of us examining evil, is evident through the ages, and is illustrated by the words of no less than Socrates himself, who stated "The life which is unexamined is not worth living"[165]. Following Immanuel Kant we as students of evil must believe it exist in an unmeasurable form, but yet we can measure its effects. Jeremy Bentham, consistent with modern day psychological learning theory, argued that human behavior was a result of avoidance of pain and the acquisition of pleasure. In the discussions below of theories of evil and explanations of its effects, we shall abide by Bentham's idea, as in our original definition (above).

Baron-Cohen[166] represents those scientists who see evil as the central trait of the psychopath, shown by the lack (or total absence) of empathy. He argues that evil can thus be explained by neuroscience, genetics, as well as environmental factors, such as early life neglect and abuse. Such an argument merges the concepts of the primary psychopath and the secondary psychopath. These two concepts approach evil behavior and the causation of the condition causing the behavior from two different perspectives and theoretical frames of reference. Psychopathy ("psychopath") is theorized to be the result of physiological factors while Sociopathy ("sociopath") results from the early and continuous ineffective parenting and inadequate socialization, the same distinctions drawn by Baron-Cohen. While critical differences between the two are theoretical, both for our purposes are "evil". The psychopath is diagnosed and handled by mental health professionals, such as clinical psychologists and psychiatrists, while the sociopath is likely to be best handled and understood by the clinical sociologist, who focuses on the force of learned norms and values (or failure to learn). Much attention in the theoretical and research literature has been devoted to these two concepts of evil. The attention to the psychopath began in earnest with the work *The Mask of Sanity* by Hervey Cleckley, first published in 1941 with multiple later editions. His treatment of the concept of psychopath includes fascination case histories of such persons. The reader is advised to read that book.

Yet, evil, while clearly personified by the sociopath and the psychopath, is not limited to the behavior of those with such causes, definitions and characteristics as are ascribed to the antisocial personality types. Indeed, much evil has been committed by persons without sociopathic/psychopathic traits as the other chapters of this book illustrate. Below we review the major theoretical explanations for evil.

Social Structure: STRAIN AND SUBCULTURE, THE SOCIOLOGY OF KNOWLEDGE, AND INSIDER/ OUTSIDER GROUPS – THE FOCUS OF THIS MANUSCRIPT

MILGRAM AND ZIMBARDO

The work of these two scientists, although done decades ago, continues to significantly influence the scientific study of evil, and the entire field of criminology/ sociology as well as other disciplines. It is unlikely we could refer the reader to a more poignant and productive body of research than obedience to authority[167] and the fabricated prison environment[168] studies. Yet, note the recent methodological critiques of the works.

Stanley Milgram, in the 1960s, advertised in a local newspaper that the Yale University Department of Psychology needed volunteer subjects for a study of learning. The responders were local, ordinary, normal middle aged men, and Milgram, a Yale Professor, was the leader of the experiment. He told the subjects they would draw straws with another subject to see who would be the "teacher" in the learning experiment and which would be the "learner". It was a set-up so that the "subject" who was picked to be the learner was always a confederate of Milgram, that is, part of a hidden experimental study. The learner and the teacher were taken by Professor Milgram to a room where elaborate electronic equipment was housed. The teacher would sit there and give the tests and when told to do so, the electric shocks. On the other side of the wall was another room where the learner would set, attached to elaborate electronic wires. The teacher watched as the Professor attached the learner to the electric wires, and the teacher was given a mild shock to illustrate it would hurt. The teacher could hear the learner from the second room but not see him. The learner stated that he had a mild heart condition and asked if it would be dangerous to get the shocks. The Professor / Experimenter told him it could be painful but would not damage his skin tissue. Then all communications between the learner in one room and the teacher in the other room were by way of an intercom. The electronic equipment with the teacher had a series of 30 switches labeled from 150 volts "Strong Shock" to 375 volts (25th level) "Danger, Severe Shock" and at the top 450 volts "XXX" indicating intense danger. The learner did not receive any shocks but the teacher did not know that, and as the learner began to "miss" answers the Professor / Experimenter told the teacher to shock the learner, at increasing levels of voltage. When the teacher pressed the switches, they gave off a harsh buzzing sound, and at 120 volts the learner went beyond grunts and yelled over the intercom the shocks were painful. At 150 volts the learner was heard over the intercom to shout "Ugh!!! Experimenter! That's all. Get me out of here! I told you I had heart trouble. My heart's starting to bother me now. Get me out of here, please. My heart's starting to bother me. I refuse to go on. Let me out."[169] The Professor / Experimenter always gave the teacher instructions to continue, as "the experiment requires that you continue" and "you have no other choice, you must go on". Then, after agonizing screams and demands to stop, above 330 volts there was only silence from the intercom. It was reasonable to assume the learner had died of heart failure. Recall the learner was in on the experiment and was never shocked.

Zimbardo's research involved a simulated prison and students randomly assigned to prison or guard roles. The speed with which the students in the "guard" role began to mistreat the students assigned to the "prisoner" role was shocking, and the level of mistreatment was horrifying. Half of the "prisoners" had to be released early because of the severe response to the mistreatment and conditions of incarceration. The experiment itself had to be shut down before a week had passed. The students used in the experiment were normal in every measured condition and were randomly assigned to the roles. They did not have a history of criminality, or any type of disability or disorder. Yet, the authors write that "at the start of the experiment, there were no differences between the two groups; less than a week later, there were no similarities between them"[170] . The description of this research is best secured from the above citation (footnote 164). Be prepared for it is frightening. Yet here we have an obligation to identify the variables studied and to review their conclusions. Some, but not all, important concepts studied include assessment of the social situation and the structure within which it functioned. They studied conformity, obedience, deindividuation, dehumanization, moral disengagement and inaction. Describing the total sample of subjects, Zimbardo describes them as follows: "When we began our experiment, we had a sample of individuals who did not deviate from the normal range of the general educated population on any of the dimensions we had premeasured. Those randomly assigned to the role of 'prisoner' were interchangeable with those in the 'guard' role. Neither group had any history of crime, emotional or physical disability, or even intellectual or social disadvantage that might typically differentiate prisoners from guards and prisoner from the rest of society...It is by virtue of this random assignment and comparative premeasures that I am able to assert that these young men did not import into our jail any of the pathology that subsequently emerged among them as they played either prisoners or guards....It is reasonable, therefore, to conclude that the pathologies were elicited by the set of situational forces constantly impinging upon them in this prison-like letting. Further, this situation was sanctioned and maintained by a background system..."[171]

The argument from the Stanford Prison and the Conformity to Authority Experiments that it is a normal human response to do as one is told, regardless of conditions, is often cited and apparently believed. Yet many analysts have criticized that interpretation and cited much research in contradiction or embellishment of that argument[172]. We believe this body of knowledge is critical to our understanding of evil, and urge the reader to review the original works cited herein. For our purposes here, it is important to recognize that the independent (causative) variables both Milgram and Zimbardo used were basic sociological concepts, and that normal people when exposed to manipulations responded with what is accepted as evil acts far more often than expected. The use of such variables, social structure at macro and micro levels and with an emphasis on the impact of norms and values, can be shown to manipulate human behavior as a powerful determinant. What is often lost in the critiques is that individual human qualities were not totally impotent. For example, Zimbardo concludes his "Lucifer Effect" book with a heavy emphasis on the heroism of some of the subjects in both experiments and citing powerful examples of human goodness in the face of harsh opposition. Such is illustrated by the work of European Christians helping Jews during the holocaust and the many acts of many people during the 911 World Trade Center disaster. Clearly, the complexity of this broad issue demands continuing research and investigation. The impact/effect of In-Group/Out-Group membership is apparent.

MERTON

One of the earliest theories produced by the Chicago School of Sociology was Robert Merton's strain theory. It argues there is a poor fit (strain) between the goals which are socially expected of us (wealth - the American dream) and the means by which we have to achieve the goals. The strain leads to deviance and sometimes crime in order to achieve the goals in other ways, or we abandon the goals entirely.

A highly germane sociological explanation of determinants of evil lies with Merton's[173] treatment of the "Sociology of Knowledge" which utilizes the variables "*insiders* and *outsiders*". This explanation is far more pervasive than psychological or medical aspects of individuals, and indeed may arguably be applied to humanity in its entirety. The theory asserts that during heightened social conflict the differences between conflicting groups become deep cleavages, so that mutual distrust is expanded greatly. This disrupts the growth and spread of knowledge in a counterproductive manner for all. Status within one's group becomes the basis for the assertion of truth and untruth, and speculation of the "undesirable" aspects of the other group. Only in-group ideas can be believed and all out-group ideas are suspect or blatantly rejected. Group values and norms are perpetuated by insiders of ascribed (that is, who you are) rather than acquired (that is, what you accomplished) status. Identification of such roles takes on distinguishable characteristics, such as dress or speech. All people occupy both insider and outsider roles as sociological variables change. It should be emphasized that rewards and punishments (consistent with psychological learning theory) accompany statuses associated with group affiliations. Such reinforcement creates the Insider and Outsider variables that Merton so powerfully theorized.

Such statuses provide privileged, and under certain circumstances, monopolistic access to various types of knowledge, or exclusion from access to knowledge. With knowledge comes power, success, status and control, so that the rule becomes "You have to be one to understand one". It is that Insider rejection of that which is Outsider that allows groups to argue for such as the Nazi ideology and racial/ethnic hate. The Insider and Outsider _assigned_ (not acquired) status thus determines the social structure so that individuals come to take on multiple statuses with overlapping demands and roles. Merton used the example of Black and White racial groups to illustrate his theory of knowledge. Thus, with little effort the conceptualization of race and racial groups in contemporary society allows the operation of the Insider and Outsider variables to be seen. The deterministic forces of the current racial groups can be seen well. Consider someone as "good" or "evil" and how they likely see themselves as Insider or Outsider members. Then consider how their behavior will be determined and associated with that self-concept, a functionally superior theory or an expanded hypothesis.

The June, 2016 issue of _Scientific American Mind_ is devoted to a review of efforts to explain "The Mind of A Terrorist", a poignant and highly relevant topic given the events around the word at this time in history. Likely, this period will be looked back upon as a unique period, certainly as it concerns the individual terrorists and the several worldwide terrorist groups. In the opinion of the writers, this publication is consistent with the In-group and Out-group theories, beginning in modern theory with Robert K. Merton (see above). The _Scientific American Mind_ report indicates, consistent with our review of the In-Group Out-Group theoretical explanations, that it is incorrect to assume those blowing up themselves for ISIS are psychopaths. Rather, they note the long history of sound experimentation going back decades, showing that normal people can do harm to others when ordered to do so. A highly respected anthropologist[174] recently wrote that terrorism comes not from "an inherent personality defect but the person-changing dynamics of the group". Such dynamics involve conflict between groups, so that attacks on the other group typically cause the other group to respond in kind, and both sides have their pre-conceived notions validated, and violent escalation continues. A normal young person, (involving Muslims, Christians and Jews) "radicalized" by the terrorist group, sociologically links with those in his In-Group and rejects the worth of those outside his group. That commitment to his group cause and his fellow group members is the primary variable explaining terrorism. Other mechanics of the group dynamics are involved, as the role of the group leaders may not be the deciding factor in whatever violence the radicalized youth may carry out. Rather, an individualized response to the group mission and goals, or "theology", may occur and be the deciding factor. We have seen this in individuals carrying out terror attacks alone, and investigation later did not show more than the radicalization. Yet work has shown that "co-radicalization" is being used by terrorists, who provoke a hostile reaction from their "Out-Group" (which could be us) and use that to show their young recruits their theology and what they (leaders of their "In-Group") said about those awful Out-Group people was right!! The terrorists are convincing the recruits that they (ISIS for example) offer a loving and supportive community In-Group that is building a noble and constructive human condition (unlike those Out-Group bums). Terrorists encourage "misrecognition" which is failure of your in-group fellow members to acknowledge your loyalty and In-Group devotion. For example, a Muslim today, with loyalty to the USA, might experience someone in authority misrecognizing him and treating him as an Out-Group extreme Muslim. Researchers have seen evidence that those situations may provoke distrust of the authorities who make an incorrect assumption, and that can build to rejection of the original values and loyalty.

Thus, what the researchers have seen and what resonates with our theoretical model is several fold. The terrorist In-Group uses violence to provoke their Out-Group (us) so that our response is suspicion and misrecognition of all who might be of the terrorist group. That drives those initially in our group away (called disidentification and disengagement from us) so that the ISIS terrorist arguments appear more reasonable. When the personal experiences of the potential recruit mesh with what the terrorist say, it is likely the individual will go over to the side of the terrorist.

How do we get the radicalized kids back to American values and away from ISIS or other terror group? A clinical sociologic group has de-radicalized over 500 kids who had gone to ISIS. They found out early that appeal to reason or presentation of flaws in the Radical Islam theology would not work. The only way they reached the lost kids was through emotional connections with family and friends. Once the Radical Islamic convert remembers positive aspects of the former life and family, other youth, previously rescued in the same way from the terrorist ideology, met as a group with the returning youth. As other youth, who had been in a similar Radical Islamic situation, began to provide an in-group support, remission began. It is better, of course, to give the youth the In-Group support initially and avoid his or her slipping off into a void where terrorist Out-Group ideas and social structure can take the recruit into their group.

A theme running throughout this manuscript is that reflected in the above explanations: the social situation and/or the social structure often overshadows all other behavioral determinants. Indeed, the joint utilization of the In-Group and Out-Group forces with the demands of the social situation, broadly defined, go far towards an explanation of many human events. This applies across times, demographics, and political conditions. Such an explanation is poignantly demonstrated by a consideration of the German people before and during the Nazi era. Many written explanations of that ideology and evil decisions were seen to rest with apparently "normal" people. Laurence Rees, in a powerful description and interpretation of the Nazi use of the "camps", reported "Perhaps above all, though, Auschwitz and the Nazi "Final Solution" demonstrate the overriding power of the situation to influence behavior."[175] The evil events occurring before and during WWII were not simply the impact of war. Rather, it involved normal people impacted by the legal structure and the social structure shaped by it. The mechanics of those developments are important for they can help the present civilization to avoid it. The structure of the government lending itself to the evil events can be seen in the growth of the Gestapo and Secret Police. The readers, those without a faint heart, should see the work of Jacques Delarue[176] who outlines in graphic detail the birth and growth of the Nazi killing machinery.

Herein we have argued for a model of evil and greed that is complex, involves substantial interaction effects, and incorporates the current theory-relevant scientific forces. Yet we maintain the most theoretically potent and empirically demonstrable variable is group membership, particularly "In-Group and Out-Group" forces. Such effects are often invisible to individuals. Even research restricted to individual-only forces recognizes that perceptions of ourselves and our perceptions, varies. The research strengthens our In/Group/Out/Group theoretical focus. A complementary conclusion is found in the work of Green (see foot note 176). The variable model we see in many analyses of the German social and political structure before and during the Nazi system is a powerful illustration of such effects. Although many analyses have addressed those human events, two are particularly important for a demonstration of the In-Group and Out-Group model. The work of Roland[177] is exceedingly germane. He reviews the various conditions in Germany after the Versailles Treaty, which dealt a harsh blow to the German government and people. Social and economic conditions were harsh and National Socialism seemed to many people to promise a way out and up. In effect, it was an In-Group promising rewards of multiple types. Many people shared a hatred of Jews (Out-Group) and a belief in the Master/Superior Aryan Race model. The National Socialist German Workers' Party offered self-pride and employment. The Nazi mass rallies helped them win the support of the ethnic Germans and initiate the Nazi policy of Gleichschaltung, that is, forcing all aspects and institutions of Germany to adopt the Nazi ideology. The inculcation of the Nazi ideology and fundamental assumptions of right and wrong involved a multitude of forms, far beyond what citizens of a democracy today would grant as even conceivable. The role of the family and religion as role models and value transmitters was usurped by the State, and family / religion were berated. At marriages and funerals, the Christian crucifix was replaced by the swastika, and Mein Kampf replaced the Bible. Groups of people held book burnings. The Law for the Prevention of Hereditarily Diseased Offspring was passed, allowing euthanasia by the state. At the same time, unemployment was being substantially reduced. The plight of "outsiders" or non-Aryan people was altered substantially, as "Out-Group" influence, particularly family, was minimized and "In-Group" influences and loyalty was given top priority. The indoctrination of the entire Aryan youth included not only racial values and norms but also unquestioning obedience to authority, often through training in youth organizations such as the Hitler Youth, separate for males and females. Rules and regulations instituted by the government were prohibiting Jews in public places and requiring adherence to National Socialism. This was obvious through the Nuremberg Laws removing citizenship from Jews and prohibiting Jews from personal relationships with non-Jews as well as eliminating them from professional and civil service posts. All of the exclusion and rebuking of "Out-Group" norms, values and identification is supported by secret World War II tapes of German POWs.[178] Prisoners of all ranks and positions were spied upon without their knowledge as they discussed among themselves their perceptions and experiences. The clear and unequivocal role of "In-Groups and Out-Groups" is apparent and supportive of our model.

An award winning doctoral dissertation from Harvard University, expanded into a book,[179] is a major source we wish to emphasize. Clearly, a vast amount has been written, in multiple forms, about WWII and the role of the Germans and the Jews. Yet, these two citations we note are of particular importance for our theoretical formulation of the dynamics of In-Groups and Out-Groups. Our second emphasized source, Goldhagen, begins his unique contribution to a sociological analysis by a comparison of normal morality and the cruel, pervasive and common assumptions underlying the slaughter of Jews by ordinary Germans. Prompted by instructions from his leaders, the head of the notorious Police Battalion 101 was told to sign a statement that his men would not steal food from the Poles. The Battalion commander, himself a "normal" German, indignantly asserted that they were men of good character, such values and honor arrived at by the men on the basis of free will, not a fear of punishment. They held honorable ideological values based on moral convictions. Such good men of "good moral character" carried out the gruesome slaughter of Jews and Poles, often in a far more cruel fashion than was required! Goldhagen writes that the Holocaust defies explanation as there is no comparable event in modern history. He argues existing social theory is unable to explain it. This was a uniquely German genocidal killing of Jews, based on conditions existing prior to the Nazis. His argument is consistent with our theory emphasizing In and Out groups, with the German culture being a massive "In-Group". Germans, as a society, had begun the move to total eradication of all Jews by a series of exclusion steps, all labeling them as an "Out-Group". Jews were excluded from social situations, cultural events, political participation and other exclusions building to genocide. Goldhagen states "...anti-Semitism moved many thousands of 'ordinary' Germans and would have moved millions more, had they been appropriately positioned -- to slaughter Jews."[180] He argues the explanation, new to the scholarly thought, is that ordinary people acted on anti-Semitism that concludes Jews should die, ought to die. This anti-Semitism is unique in that it involves a demand for great suffering and cruelty. Pain and suffering in the extreme were sought. Goldhagen describes the conditions sought and desired by ordinary Germans as "Blood, bone, and brains were flying about, often landing on the killers, smirching their faces and staining their clothes. Cries and wails of people awaiting their imminent slaughter or consumed in death throes reverberated in German ears."[181] He argues that the massive horror, a unique event in modern times, is not adequately explained by contemporary theory, and his task is to urge science to an adequate model. We intend for the "In-Group / Out-Group" emphasis we accentuate to be a critical part of that evolving theoretical model.

A description and theoretical analysis of the Nazi evil is found in the focus of "Police Battalion 101" by Christopher Browning. His work captures both a viral description of the "Jew Hunt" as well as a theoretical analyses of In/Groups / Out/Groups mechanics. He makes the powerful point that the killers were "ordinary middle aged working class men" committing atrocities caused by "pressures of a group setting". His recognition of "...group dynamics of conformity, deference to authority, role adaption and altering of moral norms".

We agree with the Greater Good Science Center, especially with their illustrations of noble actions within the Nazi party. An accepted example is Schindler's List, representing a heroic effort to save Jews from the Nazi killings in the camps. Oskar Schindler, for whom the list is named, was a Nazi business administer responsible for an important element of the war – supporting industry, employing Jewish prisoners as workers. By way of an elaborate collaboration with others, including a Jew unexplainably assigned (contrary to Nazi policy) to work with classified documents within the Krabow-Plaszow camp, the list was compiled. The regular procedure for handling Jews in that camp involved shipping them to another location for mass, cruel, killings. Schindler's list was Jews not to be transported for slaughters, but to be used as a labor force for a new Nazi project. Over a thousand Jews were thus saved from an intentional, painful death. The complexity of the collaboration required for such an effort is difficult to comprehend. It is outlined by Pemper. He acknowledges "I met honorable on both sides of the conflict".

It is with sorrow we must emphasize that our people and our government are not uninvolved in such human events, although not to the extent as were the German people. With all the prominence we place on Goldhagen's work and urge students of behavior to read it, we equally emphasize the works of Benjamin Madley and also Claudro Saunt in his description of a less expansive but equally as evil plan of action carried out by our American government, by American citizens.[182] From 1846 to 1873 the Native American population in California was reduced from 150,000 to 30,000. By 1880 the American census identified only 16,277 Native Americans in California. The events and the impetus plus political action behind that reduction is not covered in our public school curriculum yet it was based on a US law and signed by President Andrew Jackson. Indeed, the full extent of the Native American slaughter was ignored by historians till the 2016 work of Madley. There is not full isomorphism of Nazi and American events and causes. Yet, like the German situation, our citizens and taxes supported the violence. Also, while the gold rush was part of the explanation in California, the Nazis took the wealth of the Jews. Ours was as much genocide as was the Nazi action. Ours was an attempt to annihilate the Native Americans in California. We encourage the reader to see the Madley and the Saunt work.

In this manuscript we have argued for the distinctness of our theoretical approach. We have not argued our approach is exclusive, but rather among uncommon scientific models. Validating our method and our theoretical focus one finds work by brilliant scientists who utilize the same basic model as do we. Genuinely exceptional among similar works one finds that supported by the Russell Sage Foundation in the work of Douglas Massey[183]. He utilized a very wide interdisciplinary model, citing works from divergent sciences. Reviewers note this quality and also acknowledged his work's theoretical originality. In the publication[184] to which we enthusiastically refer the reader, he argues our common model is ancient and reducible to mechanisms for the allocation of material, emotional and symbolic resources. These involve the allocation of individuals to categories and the unequal allocation of the three resources noted above to such groups. He draws heavily on the work of Tilly in his theoretical formulation of durable social stratification termed "categorical inequality"[185]. Tilly's theoretical concepts involve exploitation, when one group takes from another consistent with a socially defined process of exclusion. Groups also utilize opportunity hoarding, when the more powerful group, again by way of sociologically defined exclusion, denies access to resources, often scarce and thus valuable. He argues the two variables upon which persons are judged for membership into In-Groups and Out-Groups for resource allocation as noted above, are likability or personal warmth and competence or the ability to generate resources. Massey generated a theoretically valuable model[186] consistent with our scheme. The reader is referred to the original Massey as well as our citations.

Figure Two: Massey's Stereotype Content Model

WARMTH

PITIED OUT-GROUP	ESTEEMED IN-GROUP
DESPISED OUT-GROUPS	ENVIED OUT-GROUP

COMPETENCE

Massey continues to deploy a model highly similar to ours in a highly detailed analysis of the stratification system in America. His scientific exploration, brilliant in its analysis and logical conclusions, focuses on racial, gender and income inequalities. Our concern is less on those variables than on the theoretical model he uses. The reader is referred to his work for details of his esteemed application of the model.

Sal Restivo's work[187] represents a high intellectual contribution to society thorough science, particularly social science in an interdisciplinary conceptualization. A primary focus of his 2017 work, described on his back cover as "a culmination point in the writing and thinking of Sal Restivo", involves our concepts of In-group and Out-group. Unfortunately, his atheistic arguments are flawed and he appears unable to grasp his botched grasp of critical variables. Indeed, his rejection of the possibility of forces beyond observation is in and of itself contrary to scientific principles. Yet, the fundamental premise of his theoretical conceptualizations can be seen in his emphasis on the role of sociological variables as the cause of a very wide range of human concepts, ideas, and behaviors. In that we agree with Restivo. He conceptualizes how our thoughts, ideas, concepts, and social / intellectual structures are based on a false reality and myths about free will and individualism. He links problems in the social sciences, philosophy, history of science and religion, and math as having their basis in our scientific studies.

A innovative approach to sociological analysis has been spearheaded by Thomas Gorman[188] although his analytic framework and theoretical approach are shared by others.[189] His integration of mainstream analytic analysis based on quantitative data, and long term participant observation (his life), termed auto-ethnography or personal sociology, will likely be a common component of introduction to sociology classes soon. He analyzes how social class, among other social institutions and structures, affect people over their lives and determine critical decisions and reactions. His focus is on the impact of the "hidden injuries" of groups or class. Specifically, based on his detailed examples from his own life, his example is how and why white working class people are angry at the wrong social forces and support political action that works against their own interests. He uses President Donald Trump as an example. The critical variables he uses are the connections between working-class attitudes toward education (schooling at all levels), sports, politics, and economics. For our purposes, it is important to see the close fit of his work with our emphasis on In-Group and Out-Groups. Moreover, his illustrations, abundant and personal, of positive and negative rewards, as well as positive and negative punishments stemming from group membership is critical. He shows how individuals may not be aware of their membership in groups providing rewards and punishments, and thus their integral composition in and of the world typically escapes all individuals.

As the numbers cited above show, and as anyone watching newscasts recognizes, we are at war, although it is not like past wars in regard to the mechanics of it. What should we do? Above we cite an issue of *Scientific American Mind* addressed specifically to terrorism. That report reviews several research studies germane to strategies designed to win this war. They note ways research shows the social structure and individuals' behavior can be shaped to prevent losing youth to ISIS, and specific actions our political and community leaders should take to protect us. The writers plan to reproduce those research studies, with the ideas and proposals for our politicians, and mail the copies to our Senators and Representative in Washington, as well as the President and head of Homeland Security. We encourage our readers to do the same.

Esoteric / Amalgamated / Integrated Theories

Although sometimes extraordinarily complex, a linking of various concepts / theories can lead to exceptional explanations. This is true of the work of Stephen Diamond[190] who produced one of the more esoteric, distinctive and idiosyncratic formulations of evil and its causes. His is a powerful work. He analyzes the American culture from the perspective of individual psychotherapy and psychopathology, weaving that focus into American cultural, values and norms. He formulates an argument for a coming spiritual and moral crisis. He specifies the "…destructive cycle of pathological anger, rage and violence in America…"[191] as potentially, indeed likely, destructive to a level yet unimagined unless the nation and the individuals leading our nation undertake a self-evaluation not unlike such introspection used in psychotherapy. His assessment is frightening, but likely helpful should such a national introspection occur. His work is highly recommended.

David Rothkopf[192] has produced a significant and profound sociological / criminological theory report that reads in so an engrossing manner that it is as much fun to read as a novel. It is best thought of as sociological theory and expose journalism combined. But his work is about real people and true events, in our time, impacting the readers of this book. It addresses the recent financial crisis, identifies by name individuals and organizations involved, explains the evil and greed-based events that transpired, and predicts future outcomes. Moreover, the work, stunning in its analysis and conceptualization of the critical variables, expands and illustrates the In-Group / Out-Group theoretical formulations so as to capture as never before a new concept, the SUPERCLASS. The conceptualizing of a "new" variable involves the use of existing theory and research combined in a focus on events unique to our time. Rothkopf asserts that "… something new is happening… now this is different.….a different kind of relationship.….something very important and not well understood…".[193] None of the elements of his conceptualizing are new, although the recognition of today's interaction of variables and outcomes are "…the first in-depth examination of the connections among the global communities of leaders who are at the helm of every major enterprise on the planet and who control its greatest wealth…and it is an unprecedented examination of the trends within the Superclass, which are altering our politics, our institutions, and the shape of the world in which we live…"[194]. He makes a strong case for such issues becoming the foremost and critically applied social and political science concerns of our day, and the future. He argues the quantifiable aspect of the Superclass is "power" which varies by its sources. It is no longer, as has been true through human history, largely an inherited quality. Measures of "power" in the Superclass include "wealth", "position", "access", "ideas", and a remaining historical quality "…ability to project violent force"[195]. This new global Superclass is composed of roughly 6,000 transient members who literally direct and determine the lives of the rest of humanity. The members do not operate as independent sovereigns, but utilize the links between members of the Superclass to magnify their power. It is this inequitable distribution of power, its global tentacles, and the forms/mechanisms of power that has created the new sociological phenomena that now determines the condition of humanity. The deployment of their power often lies with their ability to set agendas and priorities for all of us. They direct and assist decisions and determine the influence (power) of others, often involving membership in the Superclass. Among the egregious aspects of the Superclass is their maintenance of gender power. This is likely to be maintained as Asia takes a greater role in the global Superclass. Readers are encouraged to review his work and maintain a review of global events and the involved actors from this sociological perspective.

SUMMARY DESCRIPTIONS OF CRITICAL THEORIES

STATUS FRUSTRATION

ALBERT COHEN

Not all crime is motivated by achieving an economic reward (vandalism, for example, has no economic motive). People unable to meet middle-class aspirations lash out through criminal acts in frustration at their inability (because of outside constraints) to meet those aspirations.

ILLEGITIMATE OPPORTUNITY STRUCTURE

CLOWARD AND OHLIN

An illegal career path is available with alternative ways of achieving aspirations. It is structured several ways:

1. Career criminal - young offenders become career criminals by working their way up the ladder of an organized criminal group;
2. Conflict - subcultures which are not well-organized usually turn to violence against other similar groups;
3. Retreatist - individuals unable to engage in either of above two retreat into petty offending, alcohol and/or drugs, and other methods of negating failure.

FOCAL CONCERNS

WALTER MILLER

This theory argues that working-class males are driven to delinquency by the implicit values of their subcultures.

SUBTERRANEAN VALUES

MATZA

Humans naturally have desires defined as deviant/criminal (subterranean values) which need to surface. However, in some people they surface in a legal or seemingly legal way, such as pilfering stationary from the office (actually illegal, but is not considered deviant – "we all do it") or having casual sex on a foreign holiday. Others who are unable to carry out such acts in a more legitimate way may turn to crime.

MARXISM AND CRITICAL CRIMINOLOGY

MARX AND ENGELS

They saw crime as a way of accommodating capitalism, rather than as a rebellion against it. People commit certain crimes because they have to, not as a political act against the capitalist system, but of personal necessity. Consistent with our argument for the fundamental relevance to evil of In-Group and Out-Groups, Marxism recognizes that humans divide themselves into such groups. Critical to that explanation is the process involving wealth leading to the rulers group (bourgeois) becoming wealthy and the lower socioeconomic group (proletariat) being quite poor, by comparison. The conflict between these two groups leads to continual shifting of the membership of both groups. The process described is consistent with the ideas of Edmund Burke[196] who argued that distinct groups can reach an agreement to help one another. It is that cooperative contract of In-Groups and Out-Groups that allows society to advance.

Basically criminologists argue that social structure influences people's behavior. Taylor, Walton and Young in *The New Criminology* produce a "fully social theory" of crime (and deviance) which looks first at the origins of the deviant act, first acknowledging age old criminological factors such as ecological areas and subcultures, while arguing that they should be placed "against the overall social context of inequalities of power, wealth and authority"[197]. Engels is then echoed in the immediate origins of the deviant act, which is the individual interpretation of structural demands and reaction against them "in such a way that an essentially deviant choice is made"[198]. Finally, they describe crime as "ever and always that behavior seen to be problematic within the framework of social arrangements"[199]. In other words, crime is whatever the system deems to be crime according to its effect on the system. Change the social arrangements, and crimes of certain types will no longer happen.

LABELLING AND DEVIANCY AMPLIFICATION

Theorists arguing for labeling as a force maintain that law-breakers are not very different from the law-abiding. Most people commit deviant and criminal acts but only some are stigmatized for it. For example, a black youth wearing a hoodie may be stigmatized, but a white middle-aged businessman cheating his tax return will not. Consistent with our focus on In-Group and Out-Group we should seek to understand the reactions to and definitions of deviance, as well as the initial causes. A further cause, though, may be deviancy amplification. People labeled as deviant will see themselves as such and act as such.

SOCIAL DISORGANIZATION THEORY

SHAW AND MCKAY

Immigrants to a city move into the cheapest areas, which are in what they call the 'zone of transition' because it has a fast moving in and out rate (people move out as soon as they have enough money to do so). The population turnover creates 'social disorganization' - informal methods of social control (by the people) are lacking or absent because there are always different people there. Among some groups in the zone of transition, crime will become socially acceptable and that will be passed on to others.

DIFFERENTIAL ASSOCIATION

SUTHERLAND

A person becomes criminal if he receives an excess of definitions in favor of violating the law. Interacting with others who do break the law allows individuals to learn that behavior.

OPPORTUNITY

CLARKE

How attractive is a target? How accessible is it?

FEMINISM -

DE BEAUVIOR

It may be argued that recent times have seen a greater attention to gender inequalities than has been the case throughout human history.[200] The #metoo movement is one example. A potent and academic/philosophical treatment of this very important issue by Simone de Beauvoir is considered a landmark work. She argues, correctly we believe, that men are defined as human beings and women as females. Even Aristotle noted that "The female is a female by virtue of a certain lack of qualities".[201] De Beauvior argues that femininity is in large measure a social construct, learned by the humans born into a female body, and women must free themselves of this passivity and socially conditional value/norm. Also females must reject the notion they should be judged and live by a male standard. We believe there is much of value in her arguments and that humanity has lost a very great deal by repressing females and restricting them to limited roles. This is clearly consistent with our arguments of In-Group and Out-Group theory, and the work of Jurgen Haberman[202] who argued the qualities of a society rest on its willingness to criticize itself. He was a German who grew up under the Nazi social and political systems.

EMPATHY

BARTON-COHEN

This chapter began with a discussion of Cleckley and Baron-Cohen, as their concepts of evil are felt to be poignant and relevant to the scientific/theoretical analysis of evil. Baron-Cohen's book, ***The Science of Evil***, is a must-read for all concerned with explanations of evil and how those theoretical paths might be manipulated for our protection. He sees evil as a lack of empathy causing those at the low range of empathy to see others as objects. All humans fall on a bell curve of empathy, with the evil ones at or near Level 0 and the saints at a Level 6, or close. He defines empathy as "…our ability to identify what someone else is thinking or feeling and to respond to their thoughts and feelings with an appropriate emotion"[203]. He identifies an empathy circuit in the brain, which along with other physiological factors and environmental ones can be the "cause" of a lack of empathy. Capping off his superb analysis is a scale of empathy as a questionnaire with an empirical – numeric quotient. He also provides specific characteristics that may be used to identify a Borderline Personality Disorder, an Antisocial Personality Disorder, a Narcissist, and a Conduct Disorder. Clearly, his book is a valuable tool for clinicians, researchers and theoreticians.

PSYCHOPATHY

CLECKLEY

This theoretically groundbreaking work[204] sets forth the characteristics of those with no conscience and is a first to provide practical services to those working with psychopaths. He reported that although the psychopath may act normal, and maintain he/she is normal, actually they display clear characteristics as follows (Ibid, page 204):

1. *Superficial charm and good "intelligence"*
2. *Absence of delusions and other signs of irrational thinking*
3. *Absence of "nervousness" or psychoneurotic manifestations*
4. *Unreliability*
5. *Untruthfulness and insincerity*
6. *Lack of remorse or shame*
7. *Inadequately motivated antisocial behavior*
8. *Poor judgment and failure to learn by experience*
9. *Pathologic egocentricity and incapacity for love*
10. *General poverty in major affective reactions*
11. *Specific loss of insight*
12. *Unresponsiveness in general interpersonal relations*
13. *Fantastic and uninviting behavior with drink and sometimes without*
14. *Suicide rarely carried out*
15. *Sex life impersonal, trivial and poorly integrated*
16. *Failure to follow any life plan*

Also seen as aspects of psychopathic condition are:

17. *Lack of anxiety or guilt*
18. *Undependability and dishonesty*
19. *Egocentricity*
20. *Inability to form lasting intimate relationships*
21. *Failure to learn from punishment*
22. *Poverty of emotions*
23. *Lack of insight into the impact of their behavior*
24. *Failure to plan ahead.*

If the reader has not read ***Mask of Sanity***, by H.M. Cleckley we strongly encourage that such be done at once. He vividly portrays how the psychopath may have an idea and simply act it out without regard to the impact on others or on him/herself. His examples make this clear.

The DSM-IV describes the category "antisocial personality disorder" within which psychopathy falls, as involving at least 3 of the following characteristics.

1. *Lack of conformity to social norms (arrest typical)*
2. *Deceitfulness*
3. *Impulsivity*
4. *Aggressiveness*
5. *Disregard for human safety*
6. *Irresponsibility*
7. *No remorse*

Although research is clear that human behavior must be considered from the perspective of both genetics and environment, Oakley cites powerful research covering over 5,000 pairs of twins, including identical twins (genetically identical) and concludes "... some kids are born with a marked tendency towards evil."[205] Yet, psychopaths are not necessarily destined to be violent. Our experiences with offenders of a wide range, mirroring the reports of Oakley, are that they are remarkably unpredictable. Violence may not occur to them as a behavioral solution. Rather, a situation may suggest a behavior non- psychopaths would simply never consider, but the psychopath, without regard to the impact of his or her solution on self or others, may act in ways unexplainable by others. Cleckley presents this clearly in his multiple and detailed examples, some involving highly successful psychopaths in highly respected professions. The various personality disorders overlap, so that simple and easy identification of the genetic root of evil is difficult. Indeed, psychopaths may pass for typical, normal individuals. Oakley makes a strong case for successful people, including major leaders of major companies and countries, being psychopaths.

For a genuinely enjoyable treatment of the horrible topic of psychopathy, the reader should review the work of Ronson, presented as a trip through the "madness industry"[206]. In a manner designed to entertain as well as enlighten, the writer describes his effort to review an issue beyond mental disorders but which carries him through revealing experiences with those who deal with psychopathy. It is highly recommended.

Other psychologists have theorized regarding personality issues leading to evil. Perhaps one of the most comprehensive, and certainly one of the best analytical / theoretical / scientific works has been that of Zeigler-Hill and David Marcus[207] involving the "Dark Side" of personality theory. Their book pulls together papers by a wide variety of scientist/theoreticians so as to specify and describe both the good and the bad of the various personality constructs. For example, one paper addresses the dark side of "mood or sweet emotion", and another looks at the good and bad of "self-esteem". That work, involving an exciting conceptualization of the mechanics of personality traits as they swing, should not be missed by anyone concerned with evil, harm and criminality. It is highly recommended.

PSYCHOANALYTIC

FREUD

Although human efforts to explain evil are as old as humanity itself, few have had the impact of Jung and Freud. The reader is directed to Freud "The Psychopathology of Everyday Life" for a classic consideration of how and why people do wrong things. A more current consideration from that theoretical perspective involves the work of James Hollis.[208] He presents a powerful and elegant theoretical explanation of evil from a psychoanalytical perspective (Freud and Jung). Within the Freudian range, Hollis argues an eclectic mix of similar ideas with his central thesis being "...the human psyche is not a single, unitary or unified thing, as the ego wants to believe. It is diverse, multiplicitous and divided.... always divided".[209] Leaning on the id, ego, superego concepts of Freud, his theory is magnificent in its linkage of embellished concepts and exquisite in its treatment of the evil side of humanity. His description of the formation of evil within human identity and behavior is highly relevant to the focus of this book. His evil side of humanity, labeled as our "shadow", utilizes denial, avoidance, repression, projection and disassociation mechanisms. Our lives are a perpetual conflict and interaction of the evil within us against the moral and ethical aspects of our being. His conflict of good and evil portrayed through our life choices and behavior can be expanded from individuals to a grandiose philosophy of humanity. The reader is well advised to utilize Hollis in any explanation of evil.

He argues that much of human thought and behavior is a result of unconscious conflict between the residue of our very early learned expectations of others and our more current values. That conflict gives birth to "complexes". Such psychological pressures stem from that side of us which we dislike, indeed, reject, as they conflict with our noble qualities. Much of what we have incorporated within ourselves originated in our very first human parent/child exchanges. Because the many "complexes" of good and evil within each of us impact our human relationships as well as individual human behavior, maturity and self-control over our life path comes from recognizing and dealing with our complexes. Hollis, a Jungian analyst, labels this confronting our "Shadow". Our theoretical perspective (eclectic in nature and form) utilizes the Hollis notion of the "other" in our lives and the projection onto them of our negative and personally rejected values and norms. Moreover, we employ the same psychological / sociological mechanisms to utilize our "positive shadow". By that we mean our accumulated positive and noble traits and attributes, residing alongside our bad qualities in an unconscious condition, or what Freud would have labeled "libido" and the "unconscious". By recognizing and manipulating both our positive and negative traits, we gain control over our emotions and behavior so as to direct our life in constructive ways.

GENETIC CONTRIBUTIONS / CAUSES

OAKLEY

Barbara Oakley[210] wrote one of the more readable and scientifically relevant books showing the relevance of genetic knowledge to the present work. All the reviews of her book were not positive, in part because she used her deceased sister as an example in the book. Some readers did not feel it was a fair treatment, but the outline and discussion of genetic contributions, especially to psychopathy, were good. A reviewer's comment identifying the eclectic multi-theoretical nature of her work wrote "A magnificent tour through the sociology, psychology, and biology of evil."[211] Supported by a very wide range of scientific reports, she concludes "Thus the basic features of morality appear to be hardwired, and not a product of culture...Ultimately then, religion, education and even family may have less of an impact on our innate sense of morality than we may think:[212] Yet, others, including the renown Michael Stone, noted above, reject the concept of individuals being born evil.

BLOOM

Paul Bloom, an excellent moral philosopher / scientist, argues in a compelling book[213] that we are born with a moral sense and he demonstrates that by reference to compelling research with infants. A review of that work[214] notes that it is groundbreaking, and recommends it highly. Bloom indicates the research cited indicates babies, very young ones, have a sense of ethics that develops as they grow and interacts with other variables. His suggestions for further research are enticing. Bloom includes in his theoretical conceptualization of behavior a recognition of the impact of social groups, consistent with our formulation. Central to his formulation is his research evidence that even babies prefer in multiple ways people and conditions to which they belong, and with which they are familiar. The empirical findings he cites go far to justify policy recognition of the impact of group membership. His work is strongly endorsed, both his own empirical research and the citations he selects to buttress the impact of both the inherited, birth based morality of humans and group impacts in interaction with heredity. He carries group effects further, citing research showing it can be empirically demonstrated as existing among chimpanzees as well.[215]

Bloom's[216] research and review of the literature concludes human genetics may predispose us to the "In-Group/Out-Group" function we endorse. He indicates we "by nature" reject the Out-Group members and our "instinctive" response includes evil acts. Scientific recognition of that genetic based inclusion to divide humanity into In-Groups and Out-Groups buttresses our logic and theoretical model. He acknowledges the character of humans can lead to a new scientific mode, so as to include "good".

Personality and Clinical Psychology

This chapter has covered the traditional but negative psychological concepts, including such traits as narcissism, psychopathy and Machiavellianism. Psychology, as a social and clinical science, is expanding beyond those time honored ideas, and is well expressed in that innovative endeavor by the works of Zeigler-Hill and David Marcus.[217] They have organized a book of many chapters, each authored by different theorists/scientists, and providing graphic and scientifically laudable theory on narcissism, callousness, dominance, psychopathy, Machiavellianism, sadism, spite, sensation seeking, risk taking, distractibility, perfectionism, authoritarianism, overconfidence, emotional liability, anxiousness, depression, self-esteem, dependence and their own configuration of the Dark Side. Their assessment is that the Dark Side traits interact, and are continuous, so that we may recognize how little we understand of their birth and growth. They argue that evolution has shaped many of these traits. Much is yet to be done. Their pioneering work moves science in the direction of greater clarity of evil. The work is highly recommended to all serious students of criminology and social pathology.

Chapter Six
EVIDENCE OF GOODNESS

CHAPTER SIX

Evidence of Goodness – Causes Of Altruism And Collaboration For The Common Good –

This book and our entire project is devoted to understanding evil and greed. Yet, one cannot understand only one side of a coin, and we must identify for the reader that science addresses goodness as well as evil, both as explainable, operationalizable variables. The *Greater Good Science Center* at UC Berkeley is a critical part of this approach to goodness, and the reader is referred to their website (https://greatergood.berkeley.edu/). They have produced what is close to a comprehensive and critical review of the literature on the science of goodness.[218] Consistent with our argument regarding the science of evil, they also argue we are seeing a revolution in science. We have argued that is true because of developing scientific concern with the abstraction "evil" and revolutionary scientific models of "consciousness", while they argue for a "…revolution in the scientific understanding of human nature… deep roots of human goodness". Such a scientific transformation involves "…radical new developments in science: new evolutionary studies of peacemaking among our primate relatives; neuroscientific experiments that have identified the neural bases of emotions like love and compassion; discoveries of how hormones like oxytocin promote trust and generosity; and psychological studies of how and why people can be moved to practice kindness, even when it seems to cut against their own interest".[219] While addressing the obverse of our interest, often our dependent variable, they nevertheless indicate ways our argument is supported. In multiple ways, and multiple times, they indicate how the research backs up the role and impact of In-Groups and Out-Groups. At one point they identify such groups by the terms we use, In-Groups and Out-Groups. In their explanation of trust and mistrust, they recognize that belonging to a group creates more trust with members than with individuals from other groups. Addressing the development of morality[220] they analyze the truly amazing actions of those who helped Jews avoid the Nazis during the Holocaust. Recognizing that much research is needed in this area, they nevertheless identify four critical variables, again buttressing our arguments in this book. They cite as critical "…feelings of self-efficacy, a desire for reciprocity, a sense of group affiliation, and a wish to reclaim one's moral identity."[221] In a further discussion of groups as variables, they argue "I think that if anyone can find that thread of similarity with another person, for whatever reason, they're going to treat them as an in-group member rather than an out-group member. They're little threads, but there are so many that are available to us."[222]

Evil in Religion

More evil has been done in the name of religion that almost anything else in history. The Jews are no exception; you only have to look to the Old Testament of the Bible for the perfect examples of religious intolerance. We only have to look at Genesis when God made the creation, it was good; but Genesis goes on to say that when sin (evil) entered the world, it corrupted Creation. God wanted the people of Israel to have instructions for their social and religious life. Leviticus provided them the means to live with each other and with Him, through repeated cycles of sin, judgement, and repentance. In life we have seen human failure; but also God's response of patience and mercy through His people as His works unfold.

The kings and queens of the Bible and the kingdoms of the old world are good examples to follow and mistakes to avoid. Consider David, for sheer melodrama - gruesome murders, sexual exploits-superhuman feats of strength, a bizarre mutilation - no tabloid could offer you more. For Isaiah and other Old Testament prophets, God was clearly a God of both judgement and salvation. They knew nothing of a salvation that did not involve judgement. In fact, they saw God's judgement as a sign that He cared enough to save. God is in control of history and will not allow evil to persist forever. History is full of events and circumstances that changed the course of everything, maybe not immediately, but in the long run. The Jews and the Romans had a long, simmering dispute that turned into a revolt over different gods which the Romans brutally crushed. To this day "Masda stands as a rallying call for the nation."

The desperation of the Jews opened the way for Jewish settlements throughout the Roman world. The disciples made it a point to visit synagogues on their journeys to spread the Gospel of Jesus Christ. Intense persecution of the Jews and Christians was the best advertisement money could buy. All countries in the known world at that time discriminated against the Jews, even Christians.

Small, seemingly minor events have lead the world into a cataclysmic war more than once. Assassinations; ship sinking, surprise attacks, resources, and technology are just a few well known examples. One example that fits all of the above is England in 1940 when the Battle of Britain was beginning. The first blessing was leadership in a family of war lovers - Winston Churchill - He was born and trained to lead a crisis. Geographic location made defense a best opinion and a great naval history. Limited resources forced them to develop technology. A strong fighter and radar made fighter patrol unnecessary; thus saving fuel. Radar gave them the enemy strength and direction for interception. The love of God gave them the freedom to stand up to evil. The opposite was true when they invaded Europe and outside resources had to be built up over a long period of time. Churchill was right when he said, "If England lasts for a thousand years (1066-2066) this will be their finest hour." In 1940 the United States and the Soviet Union were not in the war. The United States was in an economic depression and selling supplies of all kinds to China, Japan, Great Britain, Italy, Spain, and Germany to jumpstart the economy. The Soviet Union was trading with Germany in the hope of a stalement in the west and in World War I.

The nation of Isaiah is the direct result of the Holocaust in Europe and the Jews are still looking for a Messiah to inaugurate God's Kingdom on Earth. On the positive side, religion describes God's unrelenting love; on the negative side, religion shows the human tendency to sin (evil).

Chapter Seven

CONCLUSIONS
WHAT DO WE DO NOW?

HOFFMAN

CHAPTER SEVEN

Conclusions - What Do We Do Now?

What is necessary to change the "irrational" economic, sociological and psychological patterns that have repeatedly led to asset bubbles, scams, and panics? How do we utilize the research regarding theological explanations of evil? Does existing research indicate which program or actions may reduce or remove evil?

From the perspective of a criminological researcher, the analysis of the nature of good and evil, the statistical and analytical portrayal of both, and our policy decisions regarding them are substantial and require serious students to review the literature at length. Yet, once the research evidence is considered relative to the theoretical, empirical and theological issues, it becomes clear the issues are broader than empirical science alone. A critically important factor is "what is next?" Laszlo has proposed that the "Big Question" and the "Bottom Line" are: "Are we entirely mortal? Or is there an element or facet of our existence that survives the death of our body?" [223] Our review of the empirical research and the philosophical ideas has lead the writers to conclude Laszlo is right regarding the most basic issue confronting us. His work, footnoted above, is described by highly credible reviewers as stating that "… overwhelming evidence is provided for the continuity of consciousness after physical death"…and "Hands down, this is the best collection of evidence from near-death experiences, apparitions, after-death and medium transmitted communications, past life recollections and reincarnation ever put together".[224] The writers agree the evidence cited is powerful and rigorously empirical, leading to either Laszlo's conclusion or to an obvious scientific enigma. After making the scientifically logical argument that the hard evidence demands an explanation, and concluding consciousness exists beyond living humans, he ends with the shattering statement that "The era of conscious immortality would mark a new phase in the history of human life on this planet. In this era we would transcend the still dominant belief system of mainstream modern science and realize that consciousness is a basic and enduring element in the cosmos and that our consciousness is an intrinsic part of it."[225] Consider the implications of Laszlo's conclusion for each of us. Recall his is a summary of a very large amount of scientific, empirical measurements. There can be only two interpretations of his conclusion, true or false. Keep in mind his references are not abstractions without a material basis, such as voodoo, but are human reports of events beyond our observation. He is not alone among scientists recognizing a fundamental, profoundly momentous and impending shift in the methodological/philosophical underpinning of science. As we note, many other credible scientists agree with him, as for example, the work of Eben Alexander[226]. He postulates an imminent shift from scientists developing a "Theory of Everything" to a "Map of Everything", incorporating our evolved materialistic physical laws and scientific methods with very new discoveries about "consciousness". Multiple scientists / theoreticians are writing that a paradigm shift in the fundamental scientific mode has arrived. Indeed, the profound nature of their argument and their premises demand a shift in our concept of humanity and the universe. This proposed new model stands in contrast to the materialistic model focused only on the physical world and what can be directly measured. One of the more compete descriptions of the components of the new model is the work of Stephen Martin.[227] His work *"The Science of Life After Death: New Research Shows Human Consciousness Live On"* merges empirical research and fascinating case histories in much detail with a historical review of the scientific method and theology. That work meshes theoretical assumptions rejected by many today as absurd, with variables of other models of that beyond the physical world, aspects of human experience thought to be myths, all so as to guide the reader (especially scientists) towards a new theoretical concept of spirit and body. This he does by reference to many of our best intellects, now and from the past. He and other similar theoreticians cannot be simply ignored. The writers of this book agree and predict we are at the beginning of a shift comparable or exceeding the Renaissance in its impact. Likely, nothing in the history of science and the human race will approach it. Our dilemma is outlined in Table one.

Table Three: Validity or Invalidity of the Prevailing Scientific Model related to research cited		
	Scientific evidence shows new model of consciousness	**Scientific evidence shows only measurable human events**
TRUE	New scientific philosophy and paradigm	Existing scientific model unchanged
FALSE	Prevailing scientific model prevails and remains	New scientific philosophy and paradigm

Victims. What do we do if we are individual victims? Although the focus of this book has not been victimology, it is important. Readers are encouraged to review Krisher's work.[228]

Conclusion # 1: Research scientists and theoreticians from all fields must consider, and react to, a new model of reality (for rejection or adoption).

Conclusion # 2: The role of "groups" as a path in scientific analysis can be emphasized for enhanced explanation.

Conclusion # 3: Evil, in its multiple forms, infests all of humanity.

Conclusion # 4: All disciplines, broadly construed, must be involved in the understanding and the control of evil.

Conclusion # 5: Social policy must be directed by and constrained by empirical research.

All readers of this volume are encouraged to respond to the conclusions above. Such response may take a multitude of forms, suited to the theoretical perspective of the reader. The authors of this manuscript will initially respond in the forms discussed below.

Response: Conclusion 1. We will request respected professionals from the relevant disciplines to serve as co-authors for a second volume on evil. The form of volume two will be determined by the group.

Response: Conclusion 2. We will request relevant professional associations and groups to take note of our work and publicly encourage a greater consideration of the variable "group".

Response: Conclusion 3. We and others will publicly recognize evil situated so as to have wide impact when originating with powerful individuals.

Response: Conclusion 4 and 5. Presently multiple groups and organizations recognize and publicize forms of evil and mechanisms for applying science as control measures. We will request our interdisciplinary group of professionals to insure everyone is informed of sources of research for policy formulation.

APPENDIX

In order to secure an unbiased indicator of the broad concepts of evil and greed, this project submitted a request for all and any persons to anonymously submit a short survey from the internet. Please note this involves a distinct methodological element, that of absolute unidentified response identity. The form that was widely distributed follows.

"Request for public help defining a social science force"

As scientists we are trying to understand "Evil" and need information from others. Such help must be anonymous to allow open and revealing statements. Please assist us by sending us your response to two simple questions concerning "Evil". Your answers must not include any information that would identify you or others. Please enter the following on the internet, to take you to our web based, *anonymous, private, no one knows who you are*, site:

https://www.surveymonkey.com/r/BKYB9GT

Do not reveal who you or others mentioned are, be anonymous only.

Upon entry of the above internet address, subject were shown the following, with a space to answer.

1. Your definition of "Evil":
2. Give an example of "Evil" you know to be true:

The responses we received follow and have not been subject to analysis. The readers are encouraged to explore this raw data.

Subject 1

Response data and time: Monday, October 30, 2017 10:43:41 AM to 10:44:22 AM

Q1: Absence of God

Q2: ISIS TERRORIST

Give your definition of "Evil".	Give a real example of "Evil" you know to be true.
Something that you would consider the absolute worst that you could imagine. Examples would be abortion, drugs, child molestation, human trafficking and the list goes on…	Drug addiction.
Evil is contrary to good and in Christendom it is generally seen as being associated with Satan.	The violent taking of innocent life, be it the ripping apart arms and legs of an unborn child (abortion) or the forcible violent act of rape, incest, or murder. Everything that is no good – is evil.
Intentional harm to others in violation of God's word.	Lies told to a "partner" in order to get sex.

I meditated upon the request stated in your letter I received a short while ago: Help Define EVIL. I had never had it come to me in such a manner before, after 60 years in ministry. This was the revelation: "Write down DEVIL and remove the (D) and you see what you get, EVIL" (the source of EVIL)"	
The absence of good	Intentional killing of an innocent person
Enmity against God.	"Thou shalt not kill" – perpetrating murder.
When you do something against God's will and it hurts other people.	Killing another human being.
Evils is taking of life without the decision of the court system. Evil is the cruelty and inhumane treatment of others.	The deadly force of the Taliban is Evil. The annihilation of the Jews as ordered by Adolf Hitler is evil.
Something that can harm anyone by any means.	Greed.
The debased thoughts of an individual that leads one to hate and/or perform acts which are harmful to others.	The evil act of a young man at a KKK rally in Charlottesville that drove his car through a crowd, killing a young woman.
Doing bad or having bad intentions.	Murder.
Demonic.	ISLAM.
Not good, not God inspired	To be deliberate in the actions that pre meditated to physically harm one or more. Such as the shootings of mass persons.

Someone knowing they are benefiting from pain, and enjoying it.	Human traffickers
Anything that is against Gods word or that knowingly harms others. It's from Satan. Actions that are done in darkness or that you wouldn't do openly. Human trafficking, selling drugs......	Pure hate and evil. Complete disregard for human life, and suffering. Or human trafficking. Such evil actions with TOTAL Disregard for anyone else.
Evil is a demonic spirit that is able to captivate the mind and create forces of destruction	When I think of evil I think of the middle passage and the evil of slavery.
Calculating and cold without feeling. Having no remorse or guilt about causing harm to others. In fact, possibly gaining pleasure from causing harm to others.	I recently read a story about someone setting a dog on fire. That is pure evil.
The killing of honest, Innocent people without reason.	The mass murder of minorities by the KKK and other like groups.
An action or behavior that ignores standard civilized behavior and serves the individuals mental or emotional satisfaction.	Sociopaths.
An act, intent, or thought to do harm to something.	An assault on an individual.
The opposite of good. That which harms others or self Vile/reprehensible.	Harming of others. Misrepresenting truth.
Anything immoral or corrupt.	School shootings.
Harm that is felt.	Actions by social/political leaders.

Psychopathic or absence of emotion when impacting another living being and harm is caused.	What we see the political leaders, especially the Democratic ones, doing to their own advantage and without helping the public.
Immoral and wicked	ISIS
Not spading or neutering any domesticated animal!	Not spading or neutering any domesticated animal!
An action or thing that is not just bad, but premeditatively negative, either given by, experienced by, or perceived by, a human.	Not killing a shark that has only been harvested for shark-fin-soup. [Unlawfully] forcing someone to submit to your (other's) will, against their wishes not to be.
Power	911
Evil is the condition or person who cares nothing for the feelings or rights of another, one who destroys completely with horrible pain any person or thing that it or he meets just to enjoy the destruction.	A person who walks into a public placer filed with strangers and kills them all just because he can.
When you do something that is immoral. When a person does something that has lifelong repercussions either to oneself or to someone else.	An example I would use is murdering or raping someone. You can't give back a life. A murder takes a physical life while a rape can take both a physical and mental life.
Absent of all that is good, bad, wicked, malevolent, sinful, criminal, immoral.	Taking another's life – murder, abortion, breaking an agreement – marriage, business.
Patterns of thinking which lead to actions/behaviors that are harmful or detrimental to oneself or others.	Last night a gunman opened fire in a country music venue killing numerous college students and a police officer.

Things that are bad and harm others or the environment, thought this may vary depending on cultural values.	Jeffery Dahmer.
Evil is manmade. Anything that becomes evil or seems evil or has been "deemed" evil has come from verbalization or actions of humans. Evil is a human weakness that can be overcome and eliminated or perpetuated (turned on or off) only by men.	Torture in any form is an evil I know to exist.
Intentionally not good.	
Wrongdoing to others.	Hurting others physically and mentally.
An act or person that is corruptive or wicked.	Narcissistic, murderer, rapist, thief, etc.
Morally reprehensible.	Murder.
Hitler	Nazi
Evil is anything that is contrary to the will of God.	When someone curses another person because they did not give them what they wanted.
Billy G.	Child trafficking.
Very bad pain to others.	Nazi final solution.

REFERENCES

Baron-Cohen, Simon. 2011. *The Science of Evil*: on empathy and the origins of cruelty. Basic Books.

Bergan, Helen. Where the money is.

Carmen Nobel: Journalist's Resources-Research on todays news topics. December 17, 2019.

CARTER, ROBERT T. 1991. Cultural Values: A Review of Empirical Research and Implications for Counseling. *Journal of Counseling & Development*. 70(1), 164–173

Cleckley, Hervey (1982). *The Mask of Sanity*. Revised Edition. Mosby Medical Library.

Diamond, Stephen A. 2009. *Is Greed Ever Good? The Psychology of Selfishness - What is the relationship between greed, evil and spirituality?*. Evil Deeds. March 25. (http://www.psychologytoday.com/blog/evil-deeds/200903/is-greed-ever-good-the-psychology-selfishness)

Golden, Marita an Susan R. Shreve. 1995. *Skin Deep: Black Women and White Women write about race*. NY: Doubleday.

Greene, Joshua. 2013. *Moral Tribes: Emotion, Reason, and the Gap Between Us and Them.* NY: Penguin Press.

Hoff, Karla. 2010. Fairness in Modern Society. Science. Vol 327. 19 March. Page 1467-1468.

BY SHELDON KRIMSKY, KATHLEEN SLOAN. 2011. *Race and the genetic revolution: science, myth and culture.* Columbia University Press

Morning, A. (2007) "'Everyone knows it's a social construct': Contemporary science and the nature of race" Sociological Focus, 40(4):436–454.

Morning, A. (2008) "Reconstructing race in science and society: Biology textbooks, 1952–2002" American Journal of Sociology, 114: S106–137.

Paul Callister Robert Didham Aug 2009 Who are we?: The Human Genome Project, Race and Ethnicity Social Policy Journal of New Zealand: Issue 36

Hollis, James. 2007. Why Good People Do Bad Things: Understanding our Darker Selves. NY: Gotham Books, Penguin Group.

Laszlo, Ervin with Anthony Peake. 2014. The Immortal Mind: Science and the Continuity of Consciousness beyond the Brain. Rochester, Vermont: Inner Traditions Publishing.

Race' and the Human Genome Project: constructions of scientific *legitimacy* PATRICIA

McCANN-MORTIMER, MARTHA AUGOUSTINOS AND AMANDA LeCOUTEUR UNIVERSITY OF ADELAIDE Discourse & Society Copyright © 2004 Thousand Oaks, CA. SAGE Publications

Miller, Arthur (Ed.). 2004. *The Social Psychology of Good and Evil.* (pp. 21-50). New York: Guilford Press.

Oakley, Barbara (Editor), Ariel Knafo (Editor), Guruprasad Madhavan (Editor), David Sloan Wilson (Editor) 2012. Pathological Altruism. Oxford University Press

Oakley, Barbara A. Evil Genes: Why Rome fell, Hitler rose, Enron failed and my sister stole my mother's boyfriend.

Pool, Robert. 2010. "The willing mind – Is there such a thing as genuine free will? Can we ever find out?" Research in Review. 2010.

Rainer, Jess. The Millennials. The Millennials: Connecting to America's Largest Generation – January 1, 2011

"Request for Public help defining a social science force." Retrieved October 30, 2017 (http://www.surverymonkey.com/r/BKYB9GT).

Sanders, Laura. 2010. " 'Women and children first ' holds only if a ship is sinking slowly – comparison of disasters suggests chivalry takes time". Science News. 117: 7. 11.

Staub, Ervin. 2010. Overcoming Evil ; Genocide, Violent Conflict, and Terrorism. First Edition
ISBN13: 9780195382044ISBN10: 0195382048

Tatum, Beverly D. 1997. *Why are all the Black kids sitting together in the cafeteria?* NY Basic Books. ISBN 0465 08361 7

Wilhelm, Mark Ottoni and Rene' Bekkers. 2010. "Helping Behavior, Dispositional Empathic Concern and the Principle of Care". Social Psychology Quarterly. Vol. 73: 1, page 11-32.

Winner of The International Society of Political Psychology Alexander George Book Award for the best book published in 2011 in the field of Political Psychology ;Winner of the Lasswell Award for distinguished scientific contribution

Zak, Paul J. 2011. "The Moral Molecule: Neuroscience and economic behavior
Why Some People Are Evil. Evil happens when people don't feel empathy"
The Moral Molecule .

Zimbardo, Philip G.. 2007. The Lucifer effect: understanding how good people turn evil.
New York. Random House

ENDNOTES

1. Christakis N.A. and J.H. Fowler, 2015. "Friendship and Natural Selection," *PNAS: Proceedings of the National Academy of Sciences*, 111 (Supplement 3): 10796-1080.

2. Bernstein, Michael J. 2015. "Ingroups and Outgroups." Published Online: 30 DEC 2015; DOI: 10.1002/9781118663202.wberen482, John Wiley & Sons, Ltd. See Stone, John. 2015. *The Wiley Blackwell Encyclopedia of Race, Ethnicity, and Nationalism*, ISBN 9781405189781 Wiley Blackwell.

3. Email ali2p9@hotmail.co.uk.

4. Javaid, Aliraza. 2015. The Sociology and Social Science of "Evil": Is the conception of pedophilia "evil"? *Academic Journals*, Vol 6 (1), PP 1- 9, February. ISSN 2141663x; see also White, Matthew. 2012.. *The Great Big Book of Horrible Things: The Definitive Chronicle of History's 100 Worst Atrocities*. NY: WW Norton and Company, publishers. ISBN 978 0 393 08192 3.

5. Rosenbaum, Ron. 2002. "Some thoughts on Hitler, bin Laden and the Hierarchy of Wickedness." February, *Atlantic Monthly*, ISSN 10727825.

6. Wang, Long and J. Keith Murnighan. 2007. *On the Duality of Greed*. Kellogg School of Management. Evanston IL 60208. see also Robertson, A. F. 2001. *Greed: Gut Feelings: Growth, and History*. Cambridge: Polity Press. ISBN074562605X.

7. Ibid, Javaid, Footnote 4, page 1.

8. Balot, R. K. 2001. *Greed and Injustice in Classic Athens*. Princeton: Princeton University Press. ISBN 9780691048550.; Heilbroner, R. L. 1980, Footnote 9 below.

9. Heilbroner, R.L. 1980. *The Worldly Philosophers: The Lives, Times and Ideas of the Great Economic Thinkers*. 7th Ed., New York: Simon & Schuster. ISBN

68486214X; Schwartz, B. 1986. *The Battle for Human Nature: Science, Morality and Modern Life.* New York: W. W. Norton & Company. ISBN 0393304450.

10. Marx, K. 1844. *Economic and Philosophic Manuscript of 1844.* Dover Books, ISBN 9780486455617.

11. Smith, Richard. 2013. *The Joy of Pain: Schadenfreude and the Dark Side of Human Nature.* NY: Oxford University Press. ISBN 978-0-19-973454-2l see also ibid Balot, Footnote 8.

12. Arendt, Hannah. 2006. *Eichmann in Jerusalem.* Penguin Books. ISBN 0143039881.

13. Stone, Michael, H. 2017. *Anatomy of Evil.* Prometheus Books. ISBN 9781633883352.

14. N.A. Christakis and J.H. Fowler, 2015. "Friendship and Natural Selection," Ibid. Footnote 1. *PNAS: Proceedings of the National Academy of Sciences*, 111 (Supplement 3): 10796-1080.

15. Bloom, Paul. 2013. *Just Babies: The Origins of Good and Evil."* NY: Random House, Crown Publishers. 978-0-307-88684-2.

16. Saari, Peggy and Aaron Sain, 2001. *Holocaust and World War II Almanac.* Cengage Cale Publishers. ISBN 0787650209.

17. Huffington, Arianna. 2003. *Pigs at the trough: How Corporate Greed and Political Corruption are Undermining America.* New York: Crown Publishers. 1-4000-4771-4-10-9.; see also Bitner, Richard. 2008. *Greed, Fraud and Ignorance: A Subprime Insider's Look at the Mortgage Collapse.* Colleyville, Tx LTV Media, LLC., ISBN 978-0-9814574-0-6.

18. See https://en.wikipedia.org/wiki/Financial crisis of 2007, %E2%80%9308

19. Huffington, Arianna. 2003. *Pigs at the trough: How Corporate Greed and Political Corruption are Undermining America.* New York: Crown Publishers.

20. Huffington, Ibid, Footnote 18, page 150.

21. Morgenson, Gretchen and Joshua Rosner. 2011. *Reckless Endangerment: How Outsized Ambition, Greed, and Corruption led to Economic Armageddon.* NY: Times Books.

22. Balleisen, Edward J. 2017. "Fraud: An American History from Barnum to Madoff". Princeton, NJ: Princeton University Press. ISBN 978-0-691-16455-7.

23. Showalter and Chris Wilson. 2016. "How the pay gap hurts women's financial security." *Time*: March 14. Page 14. (see also time.com/gap) ISBN 9780689105555.

24. Sasse, Ben. 2018. *THEM-Why We Hate Each Other-and How to Heal.* NY: St.

Martin's Press. 978-1-250-19368, page 253.

25. Ibid, Sasse. Footnote 25.

26. Bower, Bruce. 2016. "Massacre hints at early origins of war". *SN Science News Magazine*. 2/20. Volume 189, #4, page 9. ASIN: B001GDJ40S.

27. Morrow, Lance. 2003. *Evil: An Investigation*. NY: Basic Books. ISBN 0-465-04754-8.

28. Roach, Marilynne K. 2002. *The Salem Witch Trials: A Day to Day Chronicle of a Community Under Siege*. Lanham, MD: Rowman and Littlefield Publishing Group.

29. Greenwald, Anthony G. and Thomas F. Pettigrew. 2014. "With Malice towards None and Charity for Some: In-group Favoritism Enables Discrimination." October. *American Psychologist*. Vol. 69, #7, page 669-684.

30. Ibid, Footnote 29. page 680.

31. Rothkopf, David. 2008. *Superclass: The Global Power Elite and the World they are making*. NY: Farrar, Straus and Giroux Publishers. 978-0-374-27210-4. See also by the same author, *Running the World: The Inside Story of the National Security Council and the Architects of American Power*. Cambridge, MA: Perseus Books. ISBN-13: 978-1586484231.

32. Isenberg, Nancy. 2016. *WHITE TRASH: The 400 year old Untold History of Class in America*. NY: Penguin Random House. 9780670785971.

33. Sora, Steven. 2003. "Secret Societies of America's Elite." *Inner Traddione*. ISBN 15997786771.

34. Lewontin, Richard C 1972. "The Apportionment of Human Diversity". *Evolutionary Biology*. Vol. 6., page 381-98.

35. Emba, Christine. 2016. "What is White Privilege?", *News and Observer*. 1/30/16, page 17a., ISSN 26888807, OCLC 46320400; see also Grimsley, Jim 2016. "White Americans are Nearly as Blind to their Racism as Ever Before." *Los Angeles Times*. February; Bailey, Issac. 2016. "White People Love Cam, Still Judge him Differently." *Charlotte Observer*. Jan. 31. Page 31A. ISSN 23317221, OCLC 9554626.

36. McArdle, Megan. 2018. "Court Cases no Longer Black and White." *Raleigh News and Record*. July 15. Page E5; ISSN 07471858. Johnson, Allen. 2018. "Contested Waters: Why so Many Incidents at Pools?" *Raleigh News and Record*. July 15, 2018; ISSN 07471858; "Laivsnet, NC School System of Neglect." July 15. Page A4, *Star News*.

37. Krimsky, Kathleen and Sloan, Sheldon. 2011 *Race and the Genetic Revolution;*

Science, Myth, and Culture. Columbia University Press. ISBN 0231156960.

38. Washington, Harriet A. 2006. *Medical Apartheid – The Dark History of Medical Experimentation on Black Americans from Colonial Times to the Present*. NY: Doubleday. 978-0-385-50993-0.; see also Bell-Scott, Patricia. 2016. *The Firebrand and the First Lady – Portrait of a Friendship – Pauli Murray, Elizabeth Roosevelt, and the Struggle for Social Justice*. NY: Borzoi Books.

39. Herrnstein, Richard J. and Charles Murray. 1994. *The Bell Curve: Intelligence and Class Structure in American Life*. NY: The Free Press. ISBN 0-02-9146739. See also Sconing, James. 2016. "Intelligence, Genes, and Success: Scientists Respond to 'the Bell Curve.'". *Journal of the American Statistical Association*. 94.445 (1999): 335+ Academic OneFile. Web. 17 Oct.

40. Sconing, James. 2016. "Intelligence, Genes, and Success: Scientists Respond to 'the Bell Curve.'." *Journal of the American Statistical Association* 94.445 (1999): 335+. Academic OneFile. Web. 17 Oct.

41. Herrnstein, Richard J. and Charles Murray. 1994. *The Bell Curve: Intelligence and Class Structure in American Life*. NY: The Free Press. ISBN 0-02-9146739, page 509.

42. Cullen, Francis T., Paul Gendreau, G. Roger Jarjoura and John Paul Wright. 1997. "Crime and the Bell Curve: Lessons from Intelligent Criminology." *Crime & Delinquency. October, vol. 43, #4, pages 387 411.*

43. Goodnow, Natalie. 2014. https://w w w.aei.org/publication/bell-curve-20- years-later-qa-charles-murray/October 16 See also A.|Eldeas, and James Pethokoukis, "The Bell Curve" 20 years later: A Q&A with Charles Murrey. Ibid.; page 9.

44. Painter, Nell Irvin. 2010. *The History of White People*. NY: Norton and Company. 978-0-393-04934-3

45. Rehm, Barbara. 2016. Editor. *Black in America*. September, ISSN 00377333. Smithsonian.

46. Associated Press. 2018. In "Algeria, Policy of Sending Migrants to Desert Remains." *News and Record*. July 15, page 21; Fahim, Faiez and Amir Shah. 2018. Taliban Overrun Afghan Army Base. *StarNews*. Page A, ISSN 19374100.

47. http://w w w.apa.org/about/policy/mascots.pdf.

48. ASA. 2002. *Statement of the American Sociological Association on the Importance of Collecting Data and Doing Social Scientific Research on Race*. http://www2. asanet.org/governance/racestmt.html

49. Wikipedia, "Human Genome Project".

50. Kalkhoff, Will, C. Wesley Younts and Lisa Troyer. 2011. "Do others' view of

us transfer to new groups and tasks: An Expectation States Approach." *Social Psychology Quarterly*, 74 (3), page 267-290.

51. Vargas, Robert. 2011. "Being in 'Bad' company: Power Dependence and Status in Adolescent Susceptibility to Peer Influence." *Social Psychology Quarterly*. 74(3), 310-332. ISSN 01902725

52. Backer, David A. (Editor) 2016. *Peace & Conflict.* University of Maryland: Routledge Publishers. ISBN 9781857439588

53. Ibid, Footnote 52.

54. Friedman, Norman. 2003. *Terrorism, Afghanistan, and America's New Way of War.* Annapolis, MD: Naval Institute Press. 1-59114-290-3

55. Kean, T. H. & Hamilton, L. 2004. *National Commission on Terrorist Attacks upon the United States., the 9/11 Commission Report: Final report of the National Commission on terrorist Attacks upon the United States.* Washington, D.C.: National Commission on terrorist Attacks upon the United States. NY: W.W. Norton and Company. ISBN 0-393-32671-3

56. Cole, David and James X. Dempsey. 2006. *Terrorism and the Constitution: Sacrificing Civil Liberties in the Name of National Security.* NY: The New Press. ISBN 13-978-1-56584-039-6. 57; Ibid. Footnote 54, page IX. See also Lawless; Jill and Danica Kirsha. 2018. "UK police treating parliament crash as terrorism." *Star News.* August 15. Page A7, ISBN 07471858

57. Ibid, Cole, Footnote 55. page IX

58. Ibid, Cole, Footnote 55. page X

59. Wallace, Max. 2003. *The American Axis: Henry Ford, Charles Lindbergh, and the Rise of the Third Reich.* NY: St. Martin's Press. ISBN 0-312-29022-5.; see also Chambers, Beverly, 2015. *Birth, Sex, and Abuse- Women's Voices under Nazi Rule.* Grosvenor Publishing Co. 978-1-78148-353-4; see also, Garman, Steve *Where was God during the Holocaust?* Private Publication.

60. Ibid, Wallace, 2003.

61. Ibid, Wallace. 2003. Page 7

62. Ibid, Wallace. 2003 page 349

63. Bower, tom. 1997. *Nazi Gold: The Full Story of the Fifty Year Swiss-Nazi Conspiracy to Steal Billions from Europe's Jews and Holocaust Survivors.* NY: Harper-Collins. ISBN 0061099821

64. Sora, Steven. 2003. *Secret Societies of America's Elite: from the Knights Templar to Skull and Bones.* Rochester, Vermont: Destiny Books. 0-89281-959-6. (see page 8). (Ibid, Footnote 62. see footnote 33)

65. Bonner, Bill. 2017. *Follow the Money*. www.bonnerbook.com . Frederick, MD.

66. Wise, David and Thomas B. Ross. 1964. *The INVISIBLE Government*. NY Random House. Library of Congress # 64-17933. See pages 3 and 4; US Secret Service Staff. 2018. *Mass Attacks in Public Spaces -2017*. National threat Assessment Center. http://www.secretservice.gov/protection/NtAC/

67. Ibid, Kean & Hamilton, Footnote 54.

68. Belzer, Richard and David Wayne. 2012. *Dead Wrong: Straight facts on the country's most controversial cover-ups. Afterword by Jesse Ventura*. NY: Skyhorse Publishing. 978-1-61608-673-2; see also Ibid, Wise & Ross.

69. Gordon, Marcy and Matthew Perrone. 2016. "Drug Exec takes the Fifth, insults lawmakers". *The News and Observer*, 2/5/, page 10A

70. Olson, Mike. 2016. Global Risks 2016: "Conflicts of Business Interest". *Bloomberg Businessweek*. 2/22-2/28, p1.

71. Ritholtz, Barry. 2016. "Broker misconduct is worse than we thought." *Virginian Pilot*. 3/6/16. Page 4 Business Section.

72. Pitts, Lewis. 2016. "The problem with the legal profession today." The *Charlotte Observer*, OCLC 9554626, 1/31/ page 31A.

73. Thompson, Ervin. 2016. "UNC's Integrity". *The News and Observer*. February 10, page 14A; OCLC 46320400; see also Kwiatkowski, Marisa, Mark Alesia, and Tim Evans. 2016. "'A Blind Eye to Sex Abuse – How USA Gymnastics protected coaches over kids by failing to report allegations of misconduct." *USA TODAY*. Front page, 8/4

74. Adams, L. R. personal report.

75. Editors, 2004. *Journal of the American Pharmacists Association*, OCLC 715062221. March/April, cited in Graedon, Joe and Teresa. 2016. "Mistakes made in the pharmacy can be deadly". *The News and Observer*, page 2C. OCLC 46320400.75; "Survey: Doctors Aren't Always honest with Patients." Mon, 13 Feb 2012, 13:25:01. *Internal Medicine News*. http://www. internalmedicinenews. com/sear...

76. Martin A Makary, and Michael Daniel, 2016. "Medical error—the third leading cause of death in the US". *BMJ* 2016;353:i2139.

77. Fauber, John and Matt Wynn. 2018. "States seldom discipline doctors despite warnings." *USA Today*. August 20., page 1-A. For details of the "Bad Medicine Investigation" see journalsentinel.com/badmedicine.

78. Editor. 2016. "The debt resumes its growth". *The Washington Post*. Jan 21, page A16.

79. Ibid. Editor. 201680. Schechter, Harold. 1990. *Deranged – the Shocking true Story of America's Most Fiendish Killer.* New York: Pocket Books. ISBN 0 671 02545 7.

81. Ibid. page 236-237.

82. Torres, John and John Bacon. 2016. "MASSACRE - Orlando mass shooting deadliest in US history". Headline. *USA Today*, ISSN 07347456. Vol. 34, #192, Monday, June 13; Editor. 2020. *Mass Shooting in the United States.* Wikipedia.

83. Editor, 2020. "On a painful day, signs of progress". April 16, page 10. *The Virginian Pilot.*

84. Bacon, John. 2018. "Clergy abuse hotline calls "swinging after report in PA" 8/20. *USA Today.* Page 2A; "Opinion: Our View: Sexual Abuse Scandal cries out for papal leadership". page 5A; Ivan Moreno and Jeff Karoub. 2018. "Catholics consider withholding donations". August 20. *Star News.* Page A4.

85. Ibid; see also https//www.pewresearch.org/topics/religious-leaders/

86. Gecewicz, Claire. 2017. *U.S. Catholics, non-Catholics continue to view Pope Francis favorably.* Pew Research Center. January 18; for public debate regarding his veracity concerning the on-going Priest sex scandal, see *The Daily Advance* newspaper, Feb. 6, 2018, page 6, Winfield, Nicole and Eva Vergara, 2018, "Letter About Abuse Coverup Belies Pope Denial". Associated Press.

87. http s://www.huffingtonpost.com/2011/0 8/21/religion-trends-clergy-churchattendance n 929963.html; http://www.latimes.com/socal/burbank-leader/ opinion/tn-blr-me-intheory-20161101-story.html

88. Chaves, Mark. 2017. *American Religion: Contemporary Trends* (2nd edition) Princeton University Press. 9781400888375.

89. Cornwell, John. 1999. *Hitler's Pope: The Secret History of Pius XII.* NY. Viking, Penguin Group. ISBN 0670886939. (for contrary positions and reactions to the work, see https://en.wikipedia.org/wiki/Hitler's Pope).

90. Ibid, page viii.

91. Ibid, footnote 89. A detailed report of these conditions is presented in the work of John Cornwell.

92. Impoco, Jim (Editor). 2016. *Hitler.* Special Newsweek edition. IBT Media, Inc. NY. # 532016; see also Stone, Norman 1980. *Hitler.* Boston: Little, Brown and Company. 0-316-81757-0

93. https://www.yahoo.com/news/former-nazi-guard-sentenced-5-years-154504987-abc-news-topstories.html?ref=gs;_Garman, Steve M. (M.D.) *Where was God During the Holocaust?* Copies may be purchased through PO Box 1674,

Elizabeth City, NC 27906 or smgarman@aol.com. See also Greene, Joshua M. 2000. *Witness: Voices from the Holocaust.* NY: Simon and Schuster - Touchstone. ISBN 0-684-86525-4; *The Buchenwald Report,* by David A Hackett, on-line at https://www.questia.com/library/3667674/the-buchenwald-report; *Inside the Vicious Heart: Americans and the Liberation of Nazi Concentration Camps Reprint Edition* by Robert H. Abzug. 1995. (Author) Oxford University Press., ISBN-13: 978-0195042368; Perl, Lila and Marion Blumenthal Lazan. 1997. *Four Perfect Pebbles – A HOLOCAUST STORY.* New York: Scholastic, Inc. ISBN 9780062489968; Frank, Anne. 1989. *The Diary of Anne Frank: The Critical Edition,* Prepared by the Netherlands State Institute for War Documentation. New York: Doubleday; ISBN 9781101871799. Hoess, Rudolf. 1992. *Death Dealer: The Memoirs of the SS Kommandant at Auschwitz.* NY: Prometheus Books, ISBN 0879757140; See also as a disturbing experience, Warren, Andrea. 2002. *Surviving Hitler: A Boy in the Nazi Death Camps.* NY: HarperCollins Publishers, 0-688-17497-3; Gutman, Israel. (Editor). 1990. *Encyclopedia of the Holocaust.* NY: Macmillan ISBN 1579583075; visit the United States Holocaust Memorial Museum, Washington, DC.

94. Ibid, Footnote 37 above; see also http://w w w.businessinsider.com/heinrich-himmler-diary-found-2016-8?yptr=yahoo?r=UK&IR=t;

95. Walker, Mark. 1995. *Nazi Science - Myth, truth, and the German Atomic Bomb.* NY: Plenum press. ISBN 9780465011889.

96. Wiesel, Elie. 1982. *Night.* Prince Frederick, MD: Haights Cross Communications. ISBN 9780553272536. See also Garman, Steve M. (undated). *Where was God during the Holocaust?* Private publication may be purchased through PO Box 1674. Elizabeth City, NC 27909 (especially page 29); see also Rees, Laurence. 2005. *How Mankind Committed the Ultimate Infamy at Auschwitz – A New History.* NY: Public Affairs Publishing. 1-58648-303-X; see also Jaffe, Noemi. 2016. *What are the blind men dreaming?* Deep Vellium. ISBN: 9781941920367; Spiegelman, Art. 2003. *Maus: A Survivor's tale.* UK: Penguin Books, ISBN-10: 0141014083; ISBN-13: 978-0141014081.

97. Warren, Andrea. 2001. *Surviving Hitler. A Boy in the Nazi Death Camps.* NY: Harper-Collins Publishers. 0-688-17497-3. 98. Wachsmann, Nikolaus. 2015. *KL: A History of the Nazi Concentration Camps.* NY: Farrar, Straus and Giroux. ISBN 9780374118259.

99. Rees, Laurence. 2005. *How Mankind Committed the Ultimate Infamy at Auschwitz – A New History.* NY: Public Affairs Publishing. 1-58648-303-X.;

see also Buergenthal, Thomas. 2009. *A Luck Child; A memoir of surrounding Auschwitz as a young boy.* NY: Back Bay Books. 978-0-316-04340-3.

100. Nyiszli, Miklos. 2011. *Auschwitz: A Doctor's Eyewitness Account.* Arcada Publishers. ISBN 978-1-6145-011-8.

101. Helm, Sarah. 2014. *Ravensbruck: Life and Death in Hitler's Concentration Camps for Women.* NY: Doubleday Publisher. 978-0-385-52059.

102. Muller-Hill, Benno. 1998. *Murderous Science: Elimination by Scientific Selection of Jews, Gypsies and Others in Germany, 1933-1945.* Cold Spring Harbor Laboratory Press 1998. ISBN 0879695315

103. Cornwell, John. 2003. *Hitler's Scientists: Science, War and the Devil's Pact.* NY: Penguin Books. 0-670-03075-9

104. National Geographic. 2007. *Hitler and the Occult.* TV Movie.

105. Linge, Heinz and Morehouse, Roger. 2014. *With Hitler to the End: The Memoirs of Adolf Hitler's Valet.* Skyhorse Publishing. ISBN 9781602398047.

106. Editor. 2017. "The Last Surviving Nuremberg Prosecutor." *The Week.* Feb. 24, p.10; Ferencz, Benjamin. Website, benferencz.org.

107. Jacobs, Janet. 2016. *The Holocaust Across Generations; trauma and It's Inheritance Among Descendants of Survivors.* NY: NY University Press. ISBN 9781479833566

108. Ibid, Jacobs. 2016. Page 150.

109. God. Undated. *The Massacre of the Innocents.* Mathew 3:2-16. Holman Christian Standard Bible. Holman Publishers. Page 1369. ISBN 9781433691558.

110. Klein, Shelley. 2002. *The Most Evil Dictators in History.* London, England. O'Mar Books. Page 16. ISBN 184317071X

111. Dikotter, Frank. 2016. "Mao's Great Famine." *History Today,* Volume 66, #8, August; see also *The Cultural Revolution: A People's History 1962-1976,* Barnes and Nobel, 2016. ISBN 9781632864215.

112. For more elaborate descriptions of the evil people and descriptions of their actions see Provost, Gary. 1990. *Without Mercy: Obsession and Murder under the Influence.* NY: Pocket Books. 0-671-66996-6; Twiss, Miranda. 2002. *The Most Evil Men and Women in History.* NY: Barnes and Noble. See http:// unknownmisandry.blogspot.com/2011/09/creepiestfemale-serial-killers.html. White, Matthew. 2012. *The Great Big Book of Horrible Things: The Definitive Chronicle of History's 100 Worst Atrocities.* NY: WW Norton & Company.

113. This was modeled, perhaps unintendedly, after the Athenian legislator Draco and his wide-ranging and harsh code of laws.

114. Ibid, footnote 114, Twiss. 2002

115. Wootson, Cleve R. 2017. "Cannibal Couple may have Drugged, Killed and Eaten as many as 30, Russian Police Allege." *Virginian Pilot*. September 28, 2017. Page 5.

116. Ward, Vicky. 2014. *The Liar's Ball: The Extraordinary Saga of How One Building Broke the World's Toughest Tycoons*. NJ: John Wiley and Sons, Publishers. Page xvi. ISBN 9781118295311; see also Footnote 120.

117. Morgenson, Gretchen and Joshua Rosner. 2012. *Reckles$ Endangerment: How Outsized Ambition, Greed, and Corruption Created the Worse Financial of our time*. NY: St. Martin's Griffin. 978-0-8050-9120-5; see also Bitner, Richard. 2008. *Greed, Fraud & Ignorance: A Subprime Insider's Look at the Mortgage Collapse*. TX: LTV Media. ISBN 9780981457406

118. Dobbs, Lou. 2004. *Exporting America: Why Corporate Greed is Shipping American Jobs Overseas*. NY: Warner Books. 0-446-57744-8.

119. Ibid. page 1.

120. Ibid. Page 53.

121. Ibid. Page 61.

122. Ibid. Chapter 10.

123. Gasparino, Charles. 2009. *The SELLOUT – How Three Decades of Wall Street Greed and Government Mismanagement Destroyed the Global Financial System*. NY: HarperCollins Publishers. 978-0-06-169716-6.

124. Madrick, Jeffrey. 2011. *Age of Greed. the triumph of Finance and the Decline of America*. NY: Random House. 978-1-4000-4171-8.

125. Ibid. Page 403.

126. Ibid. Page 404.

127. Vennard, Wickliffe B., Sr. 1964. *50 Years of treason in 100 Acts*. Forum Publishing Company; First Edition (1964); ASIN: B000VI5PKQ; https://www.treasurydirect.gov/NP/debt/current; Petersen, Melody. 2008. *Our Daily Meds: How the Pharmaceutical Companies transformed themselves into slick marketing machines and hooked the nation on prescription drugs*. NY: Sarah Crichton Books. 978-0-374-22827-9.

128. Ibid. Footnote 127

129. Ibid. Footnote 130

130. God. *Bible*, King James Version (1983) Matthew 22: 35-40, page 957. Thomas Nelson, Inc. ISBN 0-8340-0426-7/

131. Garman, Steve M. Undated private printed book. *Where Was God During the Holocaust?* Private printing, PO Box 1674, Elizabeth City, NC 27906. Kushner,

Harold. 1981. *When Bad Things Happened to Good People.* NY: Schocken Books. 080524193-0

132. Zugibe, Frederick T. 2005. *The Crucifixion of Jesus: Completely Revised and Expanded: A Forensic Inquiry.* hardcover – April 1, NY: Evans Publishing. ISBN 1-59077-070-6.

133. Ibid. Footnote 133. See also Adams, Leon Reed. 2016. Kindle book on Amazon. *Granddaddy, is God real?* Private publication.

134. Ibid. Footnote 133

135. Collins, Father Michael. 2012. *The Illustrated Bible - Story by Story.* NY: DK Publishers, page 188-189.

136. Wright, N. T. (2006) *Simply Christian: Why Christianity makes sense.* NY: Harper-Collins. 13-9780-06-050715-2; McGrath, Alister E. 2012 (6th edition). *Christian theology: An Introduction.* Wiley Publishers. 978-1-4443-3514-9; ISBN 9780756689629.; See in God's *Bible,* Daniel 250-251 and Psalms 23, 38 and 51

137. Carus, Paul. 2008. *The History of the Devil: With 350 Illustrations.* Dover Publishing Com. Page 3. 13-978-0-486-46603-3.

138. Ibid, footnote 138.

139. Ibid, footnote 138.

140. Bell, Rob. 2011. *Love Wins: A Book about Heaven, Hell and the Fate of Every Persons Who Ever Lived.* NY: HarperCollins Publishers. ISBN 9780062049643.

141. Hoose, Phillip. 2015. *The Boys Who Challenged Hitler – Knud Pedersen and the Churchill Club.* NY: Farrar Straus Giroux.

142. John and Elizabeth Sherrill. 1971. *Corrie Ten Boom,* Washington Depot, Connecticut: Chosen Books; 0 912376-01-5; Eric Metaxa, 2011. *Bonhoeffer: Pastor, Martyr, Prophet, Spy.* ISBN 9781595551382.

143. Wray, T. J. 2014. *The Birth of Satan.* St. Martin's Press. 9781466886889.

144. http://www.churchofsatan.com/

145. LaVey, Anton. 1969. *The Satanic Bible.* NY: Avon Books. 0-380-01539-0.

146. Ibid, footnote 145.

147. Ibid, footnote 137 page 472

148. Henderson, Bobby. 2006. *The Gospel of the Flying Spaghetti Monster.* HarperCollins. ISBN 0812976568.

149. Peck, M. Scott. 2005. *Glimpses of the Devil – A Psychiatrist's Personal Accounts of Possession, Exorcism, and Redemption.* NY: The Free Press. 0-7432-5467-8.

150. Ibid. page 25.http://www.churchofsatan.com/

151. Lindberg, David C. and Ronald L. Numbers. 2003. *When Science and*

Christianity Meet. Chicago: University of Chicago Press. 0-226-48214-6;
Dembski, William. 1999. *Intelligent Design: The Bridge between Science and
Theology.* ISBN 083082314X.

152. Ibid, footnote 151.

153. https://iands.org/research/nde-research/research-news35/992-what-near-death-experiences-tell-us.html

154. Ecklund, Elaine Howard and Elizabeth Long. 2011. *Sociology of Religion,* Volume
72, Issue 3, 1 September, Pages 253–274, https://doi.org/10.1093/socrel/srr003,
Published: 16 February; see also MacCulloch, Diarmaid. 2010. *Christianity –
the first three thousand years.* London: Penguin Books. 987-0-670-02126-0;
Armstrong, Karen. 1993. *A History of God: the 4000 Year Quest of Judaism,
Christianity and Islam.* NY: Ballantine Books. 0-345-38456-3.

155. Ibid. Footnote 153.

156. Ashley, Leon and R.N. 1996. *The Complete Book of Devils and Demons.* NY:
Barricade Books.

157. Dembski, William. 1999. *Intelligence Design: The Bridge Between Science and
Theology.* ISBN 083082314X; Baron-Cohen, Simon. 2011.

158. http://www.pewforum.org/. Editor. 2019. "Opinion." *The Daily Advance.* 9/21
page A4.

159. Shreve, Jimmy Lee. 2008. *Human Sacrifice: A shocking expose of ritual killing
worldwide.* NJ: Barricade Books, Inc. 9781569803462

160. Post, Stephen G., Byron Johnson, Michael E. McCullough and Jeffery P.
Schloss. 2003. *Research on Altruism and Love: An Annotated Bibliography of Major
Studies in Psychology, Sociology, Evolutionary Biology and Theology.* Philadelphia:
Templeton Foundation Press. ISBN 9781932031324. see also Post, Stephen,
Lynn Underwood, Jeffrey Schloss and William Hurlbut. 2002. *Altruism and
Altruistic Love: Science, Philosophy, and Religion in Dialogue.* Oxford University
Press. ISBN 9780195143584. 161 Ibid., page 3. 162 Ibid, page 62.

161. Ibid, Footnote 160; See also https://iands.org/research/nde-research/research-news35/992-what-near-death- experiences-tell-us.html

162. Ibid; Lindberg, David C. and Ronald L. Numbers. 2003. *When Science and
Christianity Meet.* Chicago: University of Chicago Press. 0-226-48214-6.

163. Morrow, Lance. 20003. *Evil: An Investigation.* NY: Basic Books. 0 465 04754 8.

164. Ibid. Footnote 161. 165. 166. McGrath, Alister. 2017. *Christian theology: An
Introduction.* John Wiley and sons. 9781118869567.

165. Atkinson, Sam. 2011. *The Philosophy Book.* NY: DK Publishing.

978-0-7566-6861-7; http://www.sciencemeetsreligion.org/philosophy/scientific-materialism.php. Constance Borde, Sheila Malovany-Chevallier. 2010. *Simone de Beauvoir*. Alfred A. Knopf publishers.

166. Baron-Cohen, Simon. 2011. *The Science of Evil: On Empathy and the Origins of Cruelty*. NY: Basic Books. ISBN 978-0-465-02353-0.; see also Zimbardo, Philip G. 2007. *The Lucifer Effect: Understanding how Good People turn Evil*. NY Random House. 978-1-4000-6411-3; see also Brittle, Gerald. 1980. *The Demonologist: The Extraordinary Career of Edgar Lorraine Warner*. Barnes and Noble. ISBN 978-0-5952-4618-2. Dembski, William. 1999. *Intelligent Design: The Bridge between Science and theology*. ISBN 083082314X; Baron-Cohen, Simon. 2011. *The Science of Evil: On Empathy and the Origins of Cruelty*. NY: Basic Books. ISBN 978-0-465-02353-0.

167. Ibid. Footnote 160. See also Milgram, S. 1983. *Obedience to Authority*. New York: Harper Perennial; See Smith, Richard H. 2013. *The Joy of Pain: Schadenfreude and the Dark Side of Human Nature*. NY: Oxford University Press. A vast multitude of studies and published reactions to this pioneering scientific work are available.

168. Haney, Craig, Curtis Banks, and Philip Zimbardo.1973. "Interpersonal Dynamics in a Simulated Prison." *International Journal of Criminology and Penology*. page 69-97. See also P.G. Zimbardo, 1971. "Pathology of Imprisonment". *Society* 1972, Vol. 6 and Philip Zimbardo Craig Haney, Curtis Banks, and D. Jaffe. 1973. "The Mind is a Formidable Jailer: A Pirandellian Prison". *The New York Times Magazine*, April 8, and Zimbardo, Philip G. 2007. *The Lucifer Effect: Understanding how good people turn evil*. NY Random House 78-1-4000-6411-3; see also Brittle, Gerald. 1980. *The Demonologist: The Extraordinary Career of Edgar Lorraine Warner*. Barnes and Noble. ISBN 978-0-5952-4618-2.

169. Milgram, S. 1983. *Obedience to Authority*. New York: Harper Perennial

170. Ibid. Footnote 169; Zimbardo, Philip G. 2007. *The Lucifer Effect: Understanding How Good People Turn Evil*. NY Random House. Page197.

171. Ibid. Zimbardo, footnote 170. page 196-197.

172. Haslam SA, Reicher SD (2012) "Contesting the "Nature" Of Conformity: What Milgram and Zimbardo's Studies Really Show." *PLOS Biol* 10(11): e1001426. doi:10.1371/journal.pbio.1001426; see also Footnote 163.

173. Merton, Robert K. 1973. *The Sociology of Science – theoretical and Empirical Investigations*. Chicago, Ill. University of Chicago Press. ISBN 0-226-52091-9.

174. Atran, Scott. 2011. *Talking to the Enemy: Religion, Brotherhood, and the (Un)*

making of Terrorists. Paperback – November 29. New York: HarperCollins Publishers.

175. Rees, Laurence. 2005. *How Mankind Committed the Ultimate Infamy at Auschwitz – A New History*. NY: Public Affairs Publishing. 1-58648-303-X.

176. Delarue, Jacques. 2008. *The Gestapo: A History of Horror*. NY: Skyhorse Publishing. ISBN 13-978-1-60239-246-5; see also Greene, Joshua. 2013. *Moral tribes: Emotion, Reason, and the Gap Between Us and Them*. NY: Penguin Press.

177. Roland, Paul. 2016. *Life in the third Reich: Daily Life in Nazi Germany* 19331945. London, England: Arcturus Publishing Limited. ASIN B0356E-tXO.

178. Neitzel, Sonke and Harald Welzer. 2011. *Soldaten: On Fighting, Killing and Dying – the Secret World War II Tapes of German POWs*. NY. Simon and Schuster. ISBN 978-1-849-83948-8.

179. Goldhagen, Daniel Jonah. 1997. *Hitler's Willing Executioners – Ordinary Germans and the Holocaust*. NY. Vintage Books. 0 679 77268 5. (see especially the expansive footnotes throughout the book).

180. Ibid, page 9.

181. Ibid, page 22.

182. Browning. C. R. 2017. *Ordinary Men: Reserve Police Battalion 101 and the Final Solution in Poland*. Harper Publishing. 978-006-2303028. Madley, Benjamin. 2016. *An American Genocide: The United States and the California Indian Catastrophe, 1846-1873*. Conn: Yale University Press. 978-0-300-18136-4; Saint Claudis. 2019. *Unworthy Republic: The Dispossession of Native Americans and the Road to Indian Territory*. Norton Publishing.183. Massey, Douglas S. (2007) *Categorically Unequal: The American Stratification System*. New York: Russell Sage Foundation, 0871545853 184 Ibid.

184. Ibid, Footnote 183.

185. Tilly, Charles. 1998. *Durable Inequality*. Berkeley: University of California Press.

186. Ibid. Footnote 183. Massey, Douglas S. Page 12, Figure 1.1, *The Stereotype Content Model*.

187. Restivo, Sal. 2017. *Sociology, Science, and the End of Philosophy: How Society Shapes Brains, Gods, Maths, and Logics*. Palgrave – Macmillan. ISBN 978-1349-95159-8. (Also see https://en.wikipedia.org/wiki/Sal Restivo).

188. Gorman, Thomas J. 2017. *Growing up Working Class: Hidden Injuries and the Development of Angry White Men and Women*. Palgrave Macmillan. 978-3-319-58897-1.

189. Wegs, J. R. 1990. *Growing Up Working Class: Continuity and Change Among*

Viennese Youth, 1890-1938. Penn State University Press. ISBN 0271006374. Also see multiple references in Gorman (2017), especially Ellis, Carolyn. 2004. *The Ethnographic I: A Methodological Novel About Auto-Ethnography.* Walnut Creek: Alta Mira Press.21222 221122

190. Diamond, Stephen. 1996. *Anger, Madness and the Daimonic: The Psychological Genesis of Violence, Evil and Creativity.* NY: State University of NY Press. ISBN 0-7914-3075-8.

191. Ibid, page 301.

192. Rothkopf, David. 2008. *Superclass: The Global Power Elite and the World they are Making.* NY: Farrar, Straus and Gorrax. 13-978-0-374-27201-4 193 Ibid, page 12.

193. Ibid, book jacket

194. Ibid, page xiii

195. Ibid, Footnote 192; Atkinson, Sam. 2011. *The Philosophy Book.* NY: DK Publishing. 978-07566-6861-7. Page 173.; see also Rawls, John. 2001. *Justice as Fairness – A Restatement.* 2001. NY: Bleknap Press. ISBN 0674005112.

196. Ibid, Footnote 195.

197. Ibid, Footnote 195.

198. Ibid, Footnote 195.

199. Ibid, Footnote 195.

200. Ibid, Footnote 185.

201. Ibid, Footnote 185.

202. Haberman, Jurgen. 2008. *Between Naturalism and Religion.* Polity Press.

203. Ibid, Footnote 166.

204. Ibid, Footnote 166.

205. Cleckley, H. M. 1982. *The Mask of Sanity: An Attempt to clarify some issues about the so-called Psychopathic Personality Disorder.* Rev. Ed. Mosby Medical Library, St. Louis, ISBN 0452253411; see also Ronson, Jon. 2011. *The Psychopath test – A Journal through the Madness Industry.* NY: Riverhead Books. ISBN978-1-59448-801-6.

206. Oakley, Barbara. 2007. *Evil Genes: Why Rome Fell, Hitler Rose, Enron Failed, and My Sister Stole My Mother's Boyfriend.* NY: Prometheus Books. Page 57. ISBN 978-1-591-02580-1.

207. Ronson, Jon. 2011. *The Psychopath test: A Journey through the Madness Industry.* NY: Riverhead Books. 978-1-59448-801-6.

208. Zeigler-Hill, Virgil and David Marcus. 2016. *The Dark Side of Personality – Science*

and Practice in Social, Personality, and Clinical Psychology. Washington, DC: American Psychological Association. 978-1-4338-2187-5.

209. Hollis, James. 2007. *Why Good People do Bad things: Understanding our Darker Selves.* New York: Penguin Books. 978-1-592-40276-2

210. Oakley, Barbara. 1955. *Evil Genes: Why Rome Fell, Hitler Rose, Enron Failed and My Sister Stole My Mother's Boyfriend.* Prometheus Books: Amherst, NY. 978-1-59102-580-1; see also Rautiainen, M. 2016. "Genome-wide Association Study of Antisocial Personality Disorder." *Translational Psychiatry* (2016) 6, e883.

211. Ibid, Pickover, Cliff. Note at first of book. (see also *The Killing Trap: Genocide in the Twentieth Century.* Paperback – October 20, 2005, by Midlarsky, Manus I. ISBN 978-0-521-81545-1.

212. Ibid, Footnote 211. page 5.

213. Bloom, Paul. 2013. Just Babies: *The Origins of Good and Evil.* NY: Crown Publishers. 978-0-307-88684-2. Goodall, Jane. 1986. *The Chimpanzees of Gombe: Patterns of Behavior.* Belknap press. 0674116496 (ISBN 13: 9780674116498); see also *Us and Them Understanding Your Tribal Mind* by David Berreby, 2005, University of Chicago Press.

214. Ibid. Footnote 213.

215. Ibid. Footnote 214.

216. Ibid. Footnote 214.

217. Zeigler-Hill, Virgil and David Marcus (editors). 2016. *The Dark Side of Personality: Science and Practice in Social, Personality and Clinical Psychology.* Washington, DC: The American Psychological Association. 978-1-4338-2187-5.

218. Keltner, Dacher, Jason Marsh and Jeremy Adam Smith. 2019. *The Compassionate Instinct- the Science of Human Goodness.* NY: Norton and Co. 978-0-393-33728-0.

219. Ibid, Keltner, Dacher, Footnote 208; Ibid, Keltner, Dacher, Footnote 209; Ibid, page 241, Footnote 209, page 243.

220. Laszlo, Ervin with Anthony Peake. 2014. *The Immortal Mind: Science and the Continuity of Consciousness beyond the Brain.* Rochester, Vermont: Inner Traditions Publishing. ISBN 978-1-62055-303-9; see also Editors. 1989. "Search for the Soul." Richmond, VA: *Time Life Books.* ISBN 0 8094 6360 1.

221. Ibid. Keltner, Footnote 218, page 241

222. Ibid. Keltner, Footnote 218, Page 148

223. Alexander, Eben and Ptolemy Tompkins. 2014. *The Map of Heaven – How Science, Religion and Ordinary People are Proving the Afterlife.* New York: Simon and Schuster. IBID 97814766393.

224. Ibid. Keltner, Footnote 220.

225. Ibid. Keltner, Footnote 220.

226. Ibid. Keltner, Footnote 220.

227. Martin, Stephen Hawley. 2009. *The Science of Life After Death: New Research Shows Human Consciousness Live On*. The Oaklea Press. 978-1-892538-52-9.

228. Kushner, Harold S. 1981. *When Bad Things Happened to Good People*. NY Random House. 0805241930.